/\/\/\

SITTING BULL
War Chief of the Sioux

drawn by Sitting Bull

illustrated by Eric von Schmidt

SITTING BULL

War Chief of the Sioux

by Richard O'Connor

McGraw-Hill Book Company

New York · Toronto · San Francisco

To Mimi Laffin

Library of Congress Catalog Card Number: 68-13523

1234567890 VBVB 7543210698

CONTENTS

The boy named Slow

ONE

The Boy Named "Slow"

AT FOURTEEN the boy was named "Slow" by the members of his tribe, the Hunkpapa Sioux, part of the great Dakota Nation. At the end of a summer day in 1845, however, his name would be changed by an act of bravery, and later his new name would become a part of American history.

Slow was rather small for his age but strong and sturdy. Four years before he had killed his first buffalo. Now he wanted to achieve the aim of every young Indian boy—he wanted to become a warrior. But a boy of fourteen winters, as the Sioux elders saw it, was not old enough to consider himself a warrior.

On this summer day, in his village on the bank of the Grand River in what later became known as

South Dakota, he watched the warriors of his village ride off to meet with other men of the Hunkpapa tribe. They were forming a war party to ride out and look for their enemies of long standing, the Crow. When they found the Crows, there would be a battle, and the Sioux would make off with the Crows' horses, scalps, women, weapons, and food supply.

It was a stirring sight to the boy named Slow—the warriors mounted on their best horses, war paint streaked across their faces, their weapons and shields in hand.

More than anything else in the world, Slow wanted to join his father and ride off with the warriors. He expected that his father, Jumping Bull, would refuse him permission to go along if asked. His mother and two sisters would start crying and beg him to stay with them.

So Slow watched the warriors ride away—twenty of them from his village. They would trot over to a creek a few miles away and wait to be joined by other members of the Hunkpapa tribe. Slow waited until they were out of sight; then he jumped on the back of his horse and trotted after them.

They were all assembled at the creek when Slow caught up with them. He rode over to where his father was standing beside his horse.

"What are you doing here, Slow?" Jumping Bull asked.

"We are going too," the boy replied, meaning himself and his horse.

Jumping Bull stared at him for a moment, listened to the other Hunkpapa laughing and joking about the boy's simple statement of fact.

"Fourteen winters and the boy considers himself a man, a warrior. . . ."

"Slow? We should have given him another name. . . ."

"Let him go back and wait with the women and children. . . ."

Jumping Bull listened to all the comments and then glanced back at his only son. If Slow should be killed, there would be no other son to carry on a proud and warlike tradition. Yet should the boy be discouraged? It was a good sign that, young as he was, he was eager to join a war party.

Jumping Bull spoke loud and clear, as a leader should. "We have made enough jokes," he announced. "My son will ride with us."

The others shrugged and turned away.

To his son, Jumping Bull said, "You have a good running horse. Nothing is more important than a good horse. Otherwise how can you be first in the hunt or in battle? If we find the Crows, you must

[9]

show your bravery. You understand that, Slow?"

"That is why I am here," the boy said.

"You are too young to carry a man's weapons," Jumping Bull said, "but not too young to show that a Hunkpapa Sioux, of the Tetons, of the great Dakota Nation, is born with courage."

His father handed Slow a coup stick. This was a long stick with a feather tied to the end. It was used for "counting coup," which was an act of courage. It meant touching an enemy, dead or alive. With the Sioux, as with other Plains Indians, tribal warfare was first of all a sport. Death might be part of it, but war was a game, as jousting was for medieval knights. Touching an enemy with a coup stick was one way of keeping score. A great warrior might have many scalps dangling from his belt, he might have stolen many of the enemy's horses and women, but he was equally proud of the number of coups he had counted. When a battle began, the bravest warriors dashed ahead with their coup sticks and touched as many of the enemy as they could with the feather at the end. The killing itself was done by those men on slower horses or with fainter hearts who followed them. Counting coup against an armed enemy, after all, was at least as dangerous as fighting him hand to hand.

So the boy known until that day as Slow rode off

with his first war party, armed with nothing more deadly than a stick with a feather tied to the end.

The Hunkpapa traveled north and west for several days until they approached the Missouri River. Scouts had been riding out in all directions searching for the Crows, but they had found no sign of the enemy. It was late in the day when they went into camp behind a low hill. A scout was sent to the top of the hill to look out over the surrounding countryside. If any Crows approached, the Sioux wanted to make sure they had the advantage of surprise.

Cooking fires had just been started when the scout called down that there was something on the horizon—perhaps only a dust cloud, perhaps an approaching party of Crows. Several warriors joined him on the hilltop until the sharpest eyes among them made certain what was coming out of the west.

Crows!

An enemy war party about the size of their own was approaching at a gallop. Everyone ran for their horses, grabbed their weapons, and made ready to attack the Crows.

Slow himself, though not permitted to consider himself a warrior, was painted for battle. His war horse, gray underneath, was covered with red paint. Slow was painted a bright yellow from head to foot, and wore only a pair of moccasins and a breechclout, with a few strings of beads.

Sioux warriors did not wait for orders or form themselves in ranks as white soldiers did. They all knew what to do: fly into the face of the enemy. Orders were just a waste of breath. Besides, it was every man for himself. Those who lagged behind wouldn't be able to count coup or seize scalps.

The whole war party rode like the wind toward the Crows on the horizon. Slow, living up to his name, hadn't managed to catch and mount his horse as quickly as the others. But his gray horse was so fast it overtook the others long before they came within arrowshot of the enemy.

The Crows had studied the approaching Sioux war party. It was about equal in size to their own, but, knowing how crafty the Sioux were, they suspected another group might be hiding behind the hill. If so, they were outnumbered. Instead of waiting to find out, they wheeled their horses around and began to make a run for it.

The Sioux howled with outrage at the Crows' refusal to stand and fight. Very well, it would be a running battle.

They began to catch up with the fleeing Crows now, and Slow was in the lead, thanks to the speed of his mount. More than anything else, in that first battle, he wanted to be the first in the Sioux party to count coup, a great honor even for a seasoned warrior and unheard of for a boy just wearing his first war paint.

Slow caught up with a Crow warrior just as the latter was drawing his bow and turning to take a shot at his pursuers. Slow lashed the Crow across the forearm with his coup stick, spoiling his aim. Then Slow knocked the Crow off his horse, and a moment later the enemy was killed by a tomahawk wielded by a Sioux warrior following the boy.

The running battle was over in a few minutes, since the Crows refused to turn and fight. When it was over, the Sioux had collected a number of enemy scalps, horses, weapons, and other trophies. The victorious war party then rode for their home villages on the banks of the Grand River.

Slow, though he had killed no one, was the hero of the battle. Jumping Bull put the boy on his own horse and led him through the village in triumphant pride. The horse was painted black from mane to hoofs. Black was the color of victory and honor.

"My son has struck the enemy," Jumping Bull proclaimed to the village. "He is brave. He has counted coup in his first battle. He was the first of all to count coup. I proclaim him a warrior, and I give him a new name. Everyone, hear this. His name is no longer Slow. His name is Sitting Bull."

Sitting Bull—the name was to be written large in American history, honored above all others by the Indians of his time, hated and feared above all others by the whites of his time. Now, it is a name to rank with all those who fought for what they believed was right for their people.

He became the war chief of all the Sioux tribes, those great mounted warriors of the Western Hemisphere—as U.S. cavalry generals admitted time after time—and he led them in their greatest victory over the white man.

Even from his earliest days, Slow's people saw something extraordinary in him. Indians loved their children and watched over them just as any other people do. They were quick to notice the things about their infants that might show what kind of men they would become.

During his first few years, he traveled on his mother's back, strapped to his "baby board" or slung from his mother's rawhide saddle when the tribe was on the move.

He was named "Slow" as a baby because of his deliberate manner. Even as an infant, he studied a situation gravely before making up his mind what to do about it. When he was given a piece of food or something to play with, he didn't stick it into his mouth as most babies do. Instead he held it in his chubby hand, turning it around and looking at it from all angles, before making up his mind to eat it or play with it.

And once the baby Slow was given something, he never let it go. Sometimes, to tease him, his mother or father would give him a piece of food. Slow would study it. Then they would try to take it away from him. Slow merely stared at them and hung onto what they had given him with all his strength.

War was part of his earliest memories. The tribes of the Great Plains were always warring with each other, raiding each other's villages, and children were not spared. He learned to fear a sound like the hoot of an owl, which might be the signal of his tribe's enemies prowling outside the village and preparing to attack.

Before he went to sleep at night his mother always put moccasins on his feet, because there might be a night raid by the Crows. If that happened, he knew what to do. It was the first thing his mother had taught him. He was to run outside and hide in the

[15]

darkness until the fighting was over. If the Crows found him, they would kill him.

Also part of his first memories were the wild celebrations that took place when the men returned from a successful hunt or from a victory over another tribe. The warriors would ride through the village boasting loudly of their feats and dance through the night to the beat of the drums. We may think of Indians as people who suffered in silence, looking as though they were carved out of bronze, but that was only the front they presented to outsiders, to white men. Among themselves, they never hid their emotions. If the warriors returned in defeat, they filled the village with their laments. The women and children howled with grief over the loss of their menfolk. Joy and sorrow both were expressed openly and loudly.

The boy grew up strong and sturdy. The white man still had not come across the Mississippi in any great numbers and the tribal lands of the Dakota Nation were one great hunting ground. All kinds of game were plentiful. The growing boy was nourished on rich soup and broth, pemmican (dried meat) larded with buffalo tallow, buffalo hump, haunch of venison, bear's ribs, and all sorts of smaller game. He could not have known it, of course, but he was living in the last carefree years left to the Indians. No railroads cut through the tribal preserves, no wagon trains came bringing a hostile people with strange white faces, no soldiers rode up in blue uniforms, no traders brought cheap whiskey to corrupt the warriors and drive them to crazy deeds.

So the boy grew up to a life of complete freedom, the memory of which made him all the more bitter when that freedom ended for him and his people. At ten years of age, he was given his first pony, and that same year he killed his first buffalo. There were no schools, no work or duties to be performed by a growing boy.

He spent his days with the other boys of the village racing on foot and on their ponies, wrestling, swimming in the Grand River, climbing the bluffs above it, and hunting small game with bow and arrows.

The village often was on the move, following the buffalo and other game that were the Indians' great outdoor supermarket. That was the best part of all —the excitement of packing up the village and moving off in a column across the prairie. Away went the whole village and all its possessions—horses, pack mules, and dogs—with the warriors riding out ahead and alongside to make sure they weren't ambushed by

[17]

their enemies. Any place was home when the family's tepee was pitched and his mother's cooking kettle was set up.

At night the boy would sit around the camp fire with his elders and listen to them tell stories of what had happened to the tribe in the past. That was how history was passed down from one generation to the next. It was also how the boy, and every Western Sioux boy, learned what it meant to be a member of the greatest tribe on the Plains. The council fire was his schoolhouse. There he learned everything he would need to know. Above all else, he learned how important it was to be a brave warrior. The Sioux had no love of things they owned; they lived from day to day on the bounty of the earth. All that mattered to them was the courage of their warriors. Nothing else was worth having.

Every night of his life, around the camp fire, the boy learned that one lesson—he must grow up to be a brave warrior. Nothing else, and nothing less, was expected of him.

Several years before he rode with his first war party, a prowling Crow was killed one night just outside the village. The enemy's body was brought in, and the boys were told they must go up and touch it to show they were not afraid of death. It was his first acquaintance with what war and killing really meant.

How different it was from the way the old warriors described their battles, sitting around the camp fires! This one bloody body of a man who had been alive only a few minutes ago. Yet the boy named Slow was the first to go up and touch the body, the first to prove that he was not fearful of death.

TWO

The Warning of the Yellow Bird

SEVERAL YEARS AFTER the boy named Slow had
become the young warrior named Sitting Bull,
he was out hunting by himself on a hot summer day.
It had not been a successful hunt. All morning he
had traveled on foot over the bluffs above the Grand
River, miles from his village.

In the middle of the afternoon he climbed down
the bluffs to the river bottom, where it was cooler
and shaded by many trees.

Sitting Bull was tired and decided to take a nap.
He lay down under a tree. Before he dropped off
to sleep, however, he noticed a small, bright yellow
bird watching him from the branch of the nearest
tree. It was a yellowhammer.

The youth paid no more attention to the bird, but

[20]

went to sleep. He began dreaming of a grizzly bear. It was coming through the woods toward him—a frightening dream. There was nothing the Indians feared more than a grizzly. Only rarely could their arrows pierce the thick fur, tough hide, and heavy muscles of a grizzly bear. And if a grizzly got close enough to attack, a man didn't stand a chance. Even the bravest Sioux warrior would run from a grizzly. If he succeeded in killing one—which was very rare—he wore the claws around his neck for the rest of his life with great pride.

The dream was so frightening that Sitting Bull woke up. For several moments he lay there, halfway between sleep and wakefulness.

He had started to doze off again when he heard the yellowhammer knock twice with its bill against the trunk of the tree in which it was sitting.

"Lie still . . . lie still . . . ," the little yellow bird seemed to be warning him.

Now Sitting Bull was wide awake, all his senses alert. He lay there perfectly still, not daring to move a muscle, sensing the approach of danger. While the yellowhammer stared down at him in warning, he heard a rustle of underbrush—and suddenly his nightmare of a few moments ago became reality.

A huge grizzly loomed over him. Sitting Bull

could smell its strong odor, feel its hot breath on his face. The bear's small suspicious eyes stared down at him, as though questioning what strange creature this was lying motionless under the tree.

From tribal lore Sitting Bull knew that a grizzly would rarely attack a man who played dead.

The grizzly, swaying on its great haunches, hovered over him for what seemed like an eternity. Then, satisfied that Sitting Bull was of no interest to a bear on the hunt for a snack, the grizzly turned and lumbered away into the brush.

It was many minutes before Sitting Bull dared to sit up. He wondered about the strange dream, about the little yellow bird. The yellowhammer was still sitting on the branch nearby, with an "I-told-you-so" look in his eyes.

Sitting Bull was certain that the bird had saved his life. Even as a young man he was something of a poet. Among the Sioux a man who could compose songs, who felt himself in touch with the life of other creatures, was honored for his feelings. The bravest warrior often would recite his poems or sing his songs around the camp fire or at the Sun Dance. Such a talent only added to his fame among his people.

The yellowhammer was Sitting Bull's inspiration for his first song, which went like this:

[22]

"Pretty bird, you saw me and took pity on me,
    You wish me to survive among the people.
    O Bird People, from this day you shall always
        be my relatives!"

Until the last days of his life, Sitting Bull would
sing of the little yellow bird who saved his life, as he
believed. Living so close to nature, his people did
not think it odd that he "adopted" the birds as his re-
latives and made himself their protector. From then
on, Sitting Bull spent all of his spare time studying
the birds, their ways, their means of talking to each
other. He could imitate bird song. He believed
that he could understand what they were saying, and
many times he claimed that they warned him, as the
yellowhammer did, of approaching danger.

More and more, his people noticed that Sitting
Bull was a remarkable young man. He made up his
own mind about things, and he held onto his beliefs
just as he had clung to a morsel of food or a toy
when he was a baby. The Sioux valued a young
man who was brave, but that was taken for granted
—all Sioux were brave. If a young man were also
capable of thinking for himself, of making himself an
individual, he was valued all the more. It meant he
might be the stuff of which chiefs were made. For a
chief had to think for himself.

Earlier than most young men, he was made a

member of the Warrior Society of the Hunkpapa. By the time he was twenty he was regarded as a hero. His courage was tested one day during a battle with the Crows. He was a member of a small war party attacked by a much larger party of Crows out on the prairie. There was a running battle, but the Hunkpapa finally could not avoid making a stand. Though greatly outnumbered, they turned to fight.

Sitting Bull immediately singled out the chief of the Crow war party, though the latter was armed with a rifle. Sitting Bull had only a hunting knife in his belt.

The Crow chief fired. His bullet struck Sitting Bull, going through his left foot from his toes to his heel. Ignoring the pain, Sitting Bull leaped onto the ground, dragged the enemy chief off his horse, and killed him with the knife.

The Crows were so frightened by the death of their leader that they gave up the attack and fled.

And that made Sitting Bull more of a hero than ever among his people. The bullet wound never healed properly, and from then on Sitting Bull walked with a slight limp. Every step he took, in fact, reminded the Hunkpapa of the day he had saved the war party by killing the Crow chief and scaring off his followers. There was one further

[24]

reward for that moment of valor. Sitting Bull had recovered the Crow chief's musket and was now the only man of his tribe to carry a firearm.

By this time he had married and was the father of a son. None of the warrior fame he had gained was as important to him as his first child. It seemed to him that the boy was much like himself—grave, watchful, and tenacious.

Late in the spring of 1857 his band of the Hunkpapa were camped on the headwaters of the Cannonball River, getting ready to move off to the northwest. Like most Indians, the Sioux were nomads, who moved north with the greening of the grass from their winter quarters along the Grand River. Every few weeks they packed up their village and hauled it somewhere else. Moving always made them happy. The grass would be greener and the game thicker over the horizon.

The exceptions to the general happiness were among the older people. They knew from long experience that one place was pretty much like all the rest. On this June day, one of those a little reluctant to greet another moving day was Sitting Bull's father, Jumping Bull. All night he had been moaning in his tepee with a toothache. Bad teeth were the curse of an aging Indian's life. The tribesmen had their medicine men and their cures—many of which worked, to the amazement of white doctors—but dentistry was unknown. If you were an Indian and had a bad tooth, you were out of luck.

Sitting Bull, too, was troubled. It seemed to him that the people of his village were getting careless.

Several days before, two Crows had been seen scouting the Sioux village, but they had disappeared before the warriors could mount and take off after them. Everyone laughed it off. The Crows had been beaten so many times in recent years that they wouldn't dare attack the Sioux again. Many warriors now mocked their old enemies in songs around the camp fire, calling them frightened old women.

Sitting Bull explained his concern to Circling Hawk, his friend since boyhood and a fellow member of the Warrior Society.

"The Crows are not cowards," Sitting Bull said as they sat in his tepee the night before moving day. "They have been unlucky in the times we have met in late years. In the last big battle they lost their chief. Other times they were outnumbered by us and taken by surprise."

"Yes, that's true," the long-nosed Circling Hawk replied. "We should post more night guards, I suppose."

"We should also have scouts out during the day,"

Sitting Bull said. His broad face was grim with concern. He was still only in his twenties but he had the look of a chief, the dignity and deliberate manner of a leader. But it took many years for the Sioux to make up their minds about a man and elect him their chief.

"If we had sent out scouts the other day," he said, "those two Crows would not have got away."

"You think we will be attacked?"

"I feel it in my bones."

"Then take it up with the Warrior Society."

Sitting Bull shook his head. "No-Neck and some of the others say I have too many opinions already. Whatever I say, they oppose. It is better that I keep silent."

The next day the village packed all its possessions on horse and mule back and on the travois, the wooden A-frame dragged along by a pony, and began moving off to the northwest. There were no scouts out to look over the territory ahead of the slow procession as it moved along the dip and swell of the prairie.

Everyone but Sitting Bull and his father was in high spirits. Jumping Bull's tooth still ached. The warriors dashed around the flanks of the column, chasing each other and playing tag like children. In country like this, full of one slope after another, you

[27]

couldn't see far around you. The possibilities of an ambush were plentiful.

It came without warning.

Fifty painted, armed, and howling Crows suddenly appeared in front of them, riding down the nearest slope, less than half a mile away.

There was no time to organize a defense. Everyone flew into a panic. The pack horses took alarm and began bucking. Women and children ran around crying, making so much noise they couldn't hear Jumping Bull and the other warriors telling them to keep the horses together and lead them to the nearest high ground. The warriors, too, were caught up in the confusion and dashed around aimlessly.

The Crows struck the head of the column and quickly killed two Sioux boys who were leading the pack horses.

Evidently they had come on a horse-stealing raid and were surprised to find the Sioux village on the move. They came in closer, riding into the column, but they rode away when the Hunkpapa warriors collected their wits and began charging them.

Before Sitting Bull could ride up from his position far to the rear of the column, his father jumped on a horse and galloped off to join the fighting. Old men were expected to stay with the women and children, out of danger, but Jumping Bull simply couldn't stay out of a fight when it came so close to him.

The Crows retreated toward Cedar Creek. A running battle, broken now into many individual fights, took place in the tall grass of the prairie.

Jumping Bull chased one Crow warrior down toward the banks of the creek. Suddenly the Crow pulled up his mount, jumped off and signaled Jumping Bull to fight it out on foot—to the death. The Crow was armed with a musket. Jumping Bull had only his hunting knife. But Jumping Bull feared a toothache more than death itself. What was more glorious than dying in battle?

He leaped off his horse and started running toward the Crow.

The enemy warrior raised his musket to his shoulder and fired. The bullet struck Jumping Bull in the shoulder and almost knocked him down, but he kept running toward the Crow.

By now several other Sioux warriors had come running up and shouted to Jumping Bull that they would take care of the Crow. Jumping Bull wouldn't listen. He continued advancing toward the enemy, who dropped his musket and pulled out his hunting knife.

In a moment they were grappling. Jumping Bull tried to stab the enemy warrior, but he was not young enough or strong enough for combat with a man half his age. The Crow plunged his knife repeatedly into Jumping Bull's chest, and the old man sank to the ground. The Crow, meanwhile, had jumped back on his horse and fled for his life.

Sitting Bull came galloping to the scene just as his father died. There was nothing that could be done for him, Sitting Bull saw, except to avenge his death.

Wild with grief and rage, Sitting Bull rode after the Crow who had killed his father. He followed the enemy's tracks through the creek bottoms, across the stream, and out onto the prairie on the other side.

Several miles on the other side of the creek Sitting Bull rode the Crow down, hurled his lance, and killed him.

Then, with tears streaming down his face, he returned to the main group of Sioux warriors, who were forming up to pursue the Crows. It was a long chase across the prairie. For thirty miles they kept following them and killed off those of the enemy who could not stand the pace. No quarter was given. Ten Crows were killed before the chase was called off and the Sioux rode back to their village. There they learned that three Crow women and a baby boy had been captured when another group of Sioux struck the Crows' camp while Sitting Bull and the others were chasing the Crow warriors. According to custom, the lives of the three women and the baby would be taken in revenge for the attack.

Sitting Bull mourned his father that night in the manner of the Sioux. They did not bear their grief in silence. There was no dignity in pretending indifference when someone they loved had been taken away by death. So Sitting Bull dressed himself in rags, wore his hair loose in mourning, and walked through the village with tears streaming down his face, crying out how much he missed his father. He would not be consoled by those who said Jumping Bull would have liked to die that way, grappling with the enemy.

In his rounds of the camp, he came across the lodge where the three Crow women and the baby were being kept under guard. He knew his people intended to kill them. Suddenly it seemed to him that it was all wrong, killing the innocent. These women had carried no lances; the helpless infant had loosed no arrows. Their deaths would not ease the pain of losing his father.

He called the people of his village together and told them: "I want the lives of those Crows to be spared. Yes, let them live. They have not harmed us."

"But their men killed your father!" his friend, Circling Hawk, protested.

"And they have been killed in turn," Sitting Bull

replied. "But the women have suffered enough for something they did not cause. My father was a man, and as many of you have told me, he died as he would have wished to die. The death is his. I avenged it myself on the man who killed him. These women have no part of that. Let them live, if you would make my grief less."

The women and the baby were spared. At the end of the summer they were returned to their own people on horses that Sitting Bull had given them.

The spirit of the little yellow bird, whom he believed had saved his life from the grizzly bear, lived on with Sitting Bull and made him something more than just a great warrior.

THREE

Sitting Bull Adopts a Brother

I**N HIS MIDDLE TWENTIES** Sitting Bull already had
won the reputation among his people as the best
and wisest of the young warriors. He was now
chief of the Warrior Society, though not of the
tribe itself. Another side of his character had become evident to his people when he spared the lives
of the Crow captives. The Sioux, like most Indians
or any other people, were ruthless in war. They
killed all of the enemy they could lay their hands on.
Yet they also honored a man who could show mercy, because he exhibited something lacking in most
men. It showed that he was big enough to sacrifice
the prestige he would win by killing an enemy in the
heat of battle, in the quest for individual glory.

Later in that year of 1857, after the winter supply

of meat was brought in, Sitting Bull's tribe decided to occupy themselves before winter came by waging war on an enemy who lived far over the western horizon. They were the Assiniboine, who roamed on the other side of the Missouri River in what is now the state of Montana. Once they had been part of the Sioux Nation, but they had broken away and moved west. The Sioux now hated them as much as they hated the Crows.

It was getting close to winter when the Sioux war party started out for the Assiniboine hunting grounds north of the Missouri River. Sitting Bull wore a coat made out of a white blanket and carried both his lance and the old musket. When they reached the Missouri, they found that broad river covered with ice and snow, but they pushed on northward, hoping to find the Assiniboine in their winter quarters, not expecting a visit from their enemies at that time of year.

Sitting Bull rode along with the war party, heavy-hearted over the way death had struck at those he loved. He felt as though he must be the loneliest man in the world. That summer, not long after his father was killed by the Crow warrior, a disease had struck the village—typhoid. Almost always it was fatal, despite the best efforts of the medicine men. First his mother had died of the fever. Then his wife and the son he was so proud of. Though his two older sisters were living, both of them had married and left the family lodge some years before.

A good battle, he thought, might help take his mind off his sorrows.

Many miles north of the Missouri, just when they were about to give up hope of finding any of the enemy, Sitting Bull and his war party caught sight of an Assiniboine camp near a small river.

They did not stop to decide just how to attack the little village but rode straight for it, whooping and yelling. Battles weren't planned but were fought for the sheer joy of combat. The Assiniboine came running out of their tepees and tried to flee across the ice-covered river. Few of them escaped. Men, women, and children—all were run down and killed.

All but one boy. He had tried to escape with his family, all of whom were killed. Now he stood alone out on the ice of the river with his boy-sized bow and arrows. Nearby lay the bodies of his mother and father, brothers and sisters. He was ready to fight, though, until the Sioux killed him.

One by one, the Hunkpapa rode toward him and touched him with their coup sticks. When they had all counted coup, they would kill the boy. It was the usual thing to do.

[35]

But not Sitting Bull. He rode up just as his fellow-warriors were about to close in. The boy looked into the faces of the men surrounding him and saw no mercy beneath the war paint.

He looked at Sitting Bull just as the warrior rode up. He said just one word—"Brother."

Sitting Bull's heart melted. He had no brother of his own, no parents, no wife, or child. The boy standing there with the lances of his enemies almost touching him showed no fear, only a glimmering of hope that Sitting Bull might save him.

Suddenly Sitting Bull shouted, "Don't kill him! This boy is too brave to die!"

"He is an Assiniboine," one of his comrades pointed out. "He would grow up and become a warrior himself and kill our people. Why should we let this one live?"

"I have no brother," Sitting Bull pleaded. "Let this boy live, and I will make him my brother."

He kept talking until his fellow-warriors' blood cooled, knowing that the longer he talked the less eager his friends would be to finish off the boy. Yet he could not go against the decision of his fellow-warriors. If they said the boy must die, it would have to be so. In the end it was decided that the boy would be taken back to the Hunkpapa village and his fate debated and decided by the whole village. Taking a child of the enemy into their midst was something that had to be agreed upon by the elders as well as the warriors.

Sitting Bull hauled the boy, then eleven years old, up on his own horse and rode away with the war party, homeward to their village.

He knew that it would not be easy to persuade the people of his village that the boy should be adopted as his brother. The boy might remember all too well how his family had been killed, might bide his time, and strike against them when he was older. Sitting Bull knew all that, but he was willing to take the chance. A boy of such courage, treated decently, would turn out all right.

The argument began the moment the war party returned to the village. His people honored Sitting Bull's impulse to show mercy, but they doubted that an Assiniboine could be made into a Sioux warrior.

Sitting Bull went about persuading them to his side with his usual patience and cleverness. First he dressed the boy in fine new clothes to make him as presentable as possible and painted his face in the Sioux fashion. No one could tell by looking at him, in fact, that he had not been born and brought up in the village. Then he announced that he was giving his new "brother" the name of his own father, Jumping Bull, whom everyone had loved and admired.

Sitting Bull also gave the horses he had captured in all his recent forays to various elders. This was to show how much adopting the Assiniboine boy meant to him. Everywhere they walked in the village Sitting Bull made a point of protectively wrapping his arm around the boy. Harm this boy, the gesture said, and you harm me. And just before the tribal council was called, he served a feast to the whole village, which certainly did not make him any enemies.

At the council, his plan to adopt the boy, however, was strongly opposed by one of his fellow-warriors, No-Neck, a short muscular man whose name described him well.

"The boy is an enemy, no matter what Sitting Bull says," No-Neck told the people of the village. "We did not spare any of his family or the others we caught on the ice—why should we let him live? Is it wise to let an enemy grow up in our midst? No one can say, but if he were a Sioux boy we know very well what he would be thinking and plotting.

"The boy will say to himself, 'I will take advantage of these fools and pretend to be grateful that I am given a home by them. I will wait until I am older, until I am tall and strong and everyone has forgotten that I am an Assiniboine. Then I will strike.

I will kill and kill and kill, and then I will laugh and laugh at the fools who trusted me.'

"We can no more spare the boy," No-Neck concluded, "than we would a snake we find sleeping under a rock near the river. Kill him, I say, and be done with this woman's nonsense."

Circling Hawk, a close friend of Sitting Bull's, got up and spoke next. "We can trust Sitting Bull's wisdom as we have trusted his courage in battle. Did anyone question it when he saved us during the running fight with the Crows and killed their chief? Sitting Bull has no family. Let the boy be his family as Sitting Bull wishes."

When it came Sitting Bull's turn to present his own case, he spoke very briefly. "The boy is my responsibility," he said. "I have made him my brother, and I call him Jumping Bull after my father. If you kill the boy, you kill my brother."

The elders agreed with him. Their spokesman rose to say simply, "The wish of one of us must be the law of all others. We, the Hunkpapa, must be as one in thought and action. We say that Sitting Bull has the right to keep the boy and make him his brother."

Sitting Bull did many great things in his life but few that equaled the adoption of the Assiniboine boy. In the years to come the adoption of Jumping Bull was often to be recorded as a blessing in the Hunkpapa Picture Calendar. This was a series of drawings that told of each year's events. The year 1857 was recorded as "The Winter When Jumping Bull Was Brought Home." In the future Sitting Bull's adopted brother would become one of the tribe's great hunters and warriors. The fact that Sitting Bull spared his life became known to the boy's own tribe, and many years later the Assiniboine repaid the act of mercy in full when Sitting Bull and his people were in a tight spot.

Within a few years the Sioux had more powerful enemies than the Crows or Assiniboine to deal with. The white man, even before the Civil War, was beginning to move across the great western rivers and settle on the Indians' ancient hunting grounds. To protect the settlers, the U.S. cavalry was establishing forts, guarding roads, and riding out on patrols. Several times Sitting Bull and his band fought skirmishes with cavalry patrols. He knew from the experience of other tribes, reported and discussed around the council fires, that his tribe would have to fight an all-out war with the whites or be pushed into reservations where they would be forced to give up hunting as a way of life and where they would be taught to plant corn and to raise cattle. That had already happened to the eastern branch of the Sioux, who were closer to the advance of the white soldiers and settlers.

Sitting Bull and the Sioux were convinced that the whites meant to make them "walk the white man's road." It was a phrase the white men themselves used. And the meaning of the phrase was impressed upon the Indians by the increasing number of troops sent west to protect the growing number of settlers. Evidence of the white man's intentions was to be seen everywhere.

Neither Sitting Bull nor any of his people could bear the thought of being penned up and confined to one small area. Before the white settlers came to the Dakotas, the Sioux had enjoyed centuries of wandering in the open spaces, centuries of freedom. They saw no reason to give up their wars with the Crows and other enemies—no reason to give up the land that had always belonged to them—for the white man's benefit. To them such a confined life would be unbearably dull. No one could tell them that it would be "good" for them to join civilization, to send their children to schools, to eat more bread than meat.

At first Sitting Bull was confident that the white soldiers could be resisted. To an Indian, they were not good fighters. They were loaded down with equipment, their horses were too slow, and they always fought bunched up like frightened women.

"The white soldiers," he told his fellow tribesmen, "do not know how to fight. They are not lively enough. They stand still and run straight; it is easy to shoot them. They do not try to save themselves. Also, they seem to have no hearts. When an Indian gets killed, the other Indians feel sorry and cry, and sometimes stop fighting. But when a white soldier gets killed, nobody cries, nobody cares. They go right on shooting and let him lie there. Sometimes they even go off and leave their wounded behind. It seems they are all strangers to each other. They are not bound together as we are."

What Sitting Bull had said about the white regiments was true. They *were* formed of "strangers," many of them immigrants just arrived from Ireland, Germany, and many other European countries, who had been recruited into the army because there was little else for them to do. They did not even speak a common language as yet, and commands had to be given in German, as well as English, in many regiments. Many of these men wanted to become U.S. citizens, and army service was the quickest way to do so. Nothing was stranger to them—even to those who had fought in European armies—than being confronted by painted, feathered, half-naked "savages" who neither gave nor asked quarter in this wild country without roads or farms or any other signs of civilization.

The Indians, of course, knew that the whites were fighting against each other in what they called the Civil War. Many Indians were recruited to fight on both sides—but not the western Sioux. In the last months of the war, during the summer of 1865, the Union army moved new troops to the West even while it was fighting the last campaigns of the war. The whites were determined to keep the route to California open and to extend the railroads deeper into Indian territory.

The Union general in charge of operations in the Sioux country was Alfred Sully. He had already persuaded some of the Yankton (eastern) Sioux to go on reservations and some of their warriors to act as scouts for his cavalry. Now he wanted to make peace with the Teton (western) Sioux, of which the Hunkpapa were a tribal branch.

That summer of 1865, Sitting Bull and his village were camped on the Little Missouri with other bands of Teton Sioux. Messengers bearing peace offers arrived from General Sully, who was making his headquarters at Fort Rice, on the Missouri. General Sully wanted a truce, the right to build roads and forts in Sioux territory, and he wanted to buy tribal lands. In return the government would feed the Sioux and take care of them.

To Sitting Bull, chief of the Warrior Society and one of the recognized leaders of the Teton Sioux, it was a bad bargain. The Indians would give away everything in return for the *promise* of handouts.

He walked through the big camp, preaching against the proposed truce. "Right now other Sioux and the Cheyenne are fighting white men on the Platte. Right now white soldiers are marching into our hunting grounds from the south. They do not come in peace and they cannot be trusted. This general only wants us all to come to Fort Rice so we're gathered together and can be wiped out. Then they will take over the Black Hills, our sacred lands, the land of the Great Manitou."

Many Sioux wanted to trust the white man, and Sitting Bull had to plead for time before the truce offer was accepted or turned down. Sitting Bull's proposal was that they should test General Sully's good intentions. The general was supposed to be waiting to hear from them in an Indian camp on the Missouri. If General Sully were still there, it would mean—just possibly—that he could be trusted. If he wasn't, it meant that he had slipped away to the other side of the Missouri to bring up troops and break the proposed truce the moment the Teton Sioux showed up. They would all be tricked into a slaughter.

Many Sioux were willing to trust "Grandfather," their name for the whites' government, and agreed to the test. Sitting Bull and a large band of followers rode for General Sully's camp on the Missouri. They found it deserted. The white general had slipped away on his steamboat.

When Sitting Bull rode back to the Teton camp with that news, all talk of truce ended. It was war to the end. Sitting Bull himself never wavered from that course.

Early that September he went out on the hunt for enemies along the Powder River with a war party of 400, the largest party ever formed under his leadership. He was now recognized as the wisest and most determined among the young Sioux, chief of all the Hunkpapa warriors, at the age of thirty-four.

Sitting Bull and his war party found they weren't the first to arrive on the banks of the Powder River. Already camped there were General Patrick E. Connor and hundreds of white cavalrymen. The general was determined to clear all hostile Indians out of the Powder River country. He had issued orders reading that his officers were "not to receive overtures of peace or submission from Indians." His troops were ordered to "kill every male Indian over the age of twelve," whether he offered resistance or not.

Sitting Bull sent two of his braves to the white soldiers' camp to trade for tobacco, and they were fired upon, then chased away even though they went with peaceful intentions. Sitting Bull was enraged. He ordered an immediate attack on the cavalry camp, and his warriors surrounded it. A large number of the cavalry came charging out and were lured away, over the plains, by some of Sitting Bull's men who pretended to be fleeing from them. Then Sitting Bull attacked the main body with the rest of his warriors. They inflicted heavy casualties on the whites, who soon dismounted and fought from behind fallen logs in the timber along the river.

To the Sioux, this was a coward's way of fighting. They dared the white soldiers to come out and fight in the open. General Connor's cavalry, however, wisely stayed under cover. Sitting Bull wouldn't let his warriors dismount and charge into the timber because he knew many of them would be killed by the whites' greatly superior firepower.

He and most of his 400 followers withdrew after a day of fighting. It wasn't a victory for Sitting Bull, but it was definitely a defeat for General Connor. The general was soon removed from his command. But what of Sitting Bull—was his star on the rise or on the wane?

Sitting Bull becomes the Itanchan

FOUR

Sitting Bull Becomes the Itanchan

THE VARIOUS Sioux tribes were always very care-
ful about choosing their chiefs. It was not
enough for a man to be the war chief, the leader of
the Warrior Society, as Sitting Bull was. He must
show that he was not only brave but wise and generous and large-hearted. He must be capable of for-
giveness, must never lose his temper, must share what
he gained in booty with those who had little. He
had to be literally the "father"of his tribe.

When a young man was believed to have shown
those qualities as a war chief, he was proposed for
chief of the whole tribe by the Warrior Society.
Then he would be passed upon by the council of
elders. If the old men decided that he was good

[49]

enough to lead his people in peace as well as in war, he was elected the Itanchan, the chief of chiefs.

This happened to Sitting Bull when he was about thirty-five years old. For some years the Hunkpapa had been ruled by four different chiefs, who were supposed to cooperate with each other. In recent years they had taken to quarreling with each other, and the elders decided they must be replaced. This time one chief would be elected to head the entire tribe of the Hunkpapa.

There were long meetings of the elders' council to decide on who would replace the four quarreling chiefs. Actually there was only one candidate—Sitting Bull—but the elders were concerned by the fact that he was very young to be a supreme chief. They pondered everything that was known about him: the help he gave old women and children, his lack of arrogance, his poetic and mystic side, his adoption of Jumping Bull, his sparing of the Crow captives, and his brilliant leadership of the war parties, particularly the battle with the Crows in which he had killed their chief and been wounded in the foot. Above all, of course, was Sitting Bull's deliberate way of acting. He rarely did anything on the spur of the moment. He thought things out. Furthermore, he was utterly determined not to trade away the tribal lands or give way to the whites, wherever and whenever it was possible to resist them.

Yes, the elders decided, there was no other man who could rule the Hunkpapa but Sitting Bull.

Less than a year later, in 1867, all the tribes of the Teton Sioux decided that there must be one chief for the whole Dakota Nation. They must all unite, and for that they would need one leader. Again, the man chosen was Sitting Bull. Through all the widely scattered villages of the Sioux people his name had become known for all that was good and admirable in a Sioux warrior. One of the few white men who knew him at this time was Frank Grouard, the son of a white man and an Hawaiian, who was a U.S. mail carrier. "The bucks admired him," Grouard said, "the squaws admired him, and the children loved him. He would have proved a mighty power among our politicians—a great vote-getter with the people."

Sitting Bull was installed as war chief of all the Teton Sioux at ceremonies that took many days, with all the Teton tribes camped around the big lodge. The Hunkpapa, the Minniconjou, the Oglala, the Sans Arc, and some of the Yankton and Blackfeet Sioux were there.

The ceremony took place with all the prescribed ritual. Sitting Bull was dressed in a buffalo robe and wore two feathers in his hair. He sat in a circle with all the elders and subchiefs as the long pipe passed from mouth to mouth around the circle. Each man took a puff of smoke and exhaled it with a prayer. Then Sitting Bull was presented with a ceremonial war bonnet, a headdress that stretched to the ground and was made of ermine tails and eagle feathers. Each feather represented a brave deed performed by the warrior who contributed it to the bonnet. Sitting Bull was also given a fine white horse. He mounted it and then led a procession of all the subchiefs through the great encampment of the Teton Sioux.

To all the people he now represented and led, he sang a song he had composed for the occasion:

> "Young men, help me . . . help me
> I love my people so—
> That is why I am fighting."

He also told his people that he would not attack white settlements as Indians elsewhere were doing, but he would resist their attempts to move into Sioux country and would chase out all white men but those who came to trade.

Soon after he became the supreme chief, a Jesuit missionary named Father Jean Pierre de Smet, whom Sitting Bull always called "Black Robe," came to Sit-

Father DeSmet

ting Bull's village on a peace mission. He brought with him proposals from the U.S. government and sent a messenger to Sitting Bull to ask whether the chief would be willing to talk to him.

"Tell Black Robe we shall meet him and his friends with arms stretched out," Sitting Bull said. "No man living can remember that I ever treated a peace commission with contempt, or gave them hard words. Say to Black Robe, 'We have made room for you in our hearts. You shall have food and water, and return with a glad heart. We wish to shake your hand, and to hear your good words. Fear nothing.' "

Then and always, Sitting Bull was determined to avoid fighting if possible. He was willing to live in peace with the white men if they would leave his people alone. To bring that about, he gladly talked to the white men if he was convinced that they, too, wanted peace and not merely another chunk of the Indians' freedom.

Four thousand Tetons were camped on the grassy plain in the forks between the Powder and Yellowstone rivers when Father de Smet arrived for the conference. Sitting Bull and his chiefs rode out to escort the missionary into their camp.

Riding up to greet Father de Smet, one of Sitting Bull's subchiefs, White Gut, muttered to the others,

"Here comes another white man to cheat us." Tension mounted as White Gut urged that they kill the missionary and be done with it. But Sitting Bull calmed him down.

A great lodge had been built for the meeting, and there Sitting Bull talked with the man sent from Washington, from "Grandfather," as Sitting Bull called the U.S. government, during the last days of May, 1867.

"Your Grandfather," Father de Smet told him, "wishes you to live among your people on your own lands. You will never starve. You will always have plenty of rations. You will not be captives. You will receive warm clothing."

"It sounds good," Sitting Bull replied, determined not to be misled by any of the Grandfather's promises, "but I am satisfied with the old treaty if the whites would keep it."

He wanted the missionary to carry back a message to Washington, for Grandfather: "I want only traders, no soldiers on my land. God gave us this land, and we are at home here. I will not have my people robbed. We can live if we can keep our Black Hills." The Black Hills, of course, was the sacred territory of the chief god of the Sioux, the Great Manitou. "We do not want to eat from the hand of the Grandfather. We can feed ourselves."

Sitting Bull and the white missionary talked for two days and two nights. There was good will on both sides. The trouble was that Grandfather wanted the Indians' land and in return could offer only "peace," on the government's own terms and the promise of food, clothing, and shelter. (That promise was rarely kept, as the Indians already knew. Dishonest agents of the government withheld such things and sold them for their own profit.) The Sioux also wanted peace, but not at the cost of their freedom. That issue was what kept Sitting Bull fighting for years on behalf of his people.

Father de Smet begged Sitting Bull and his followers to "bury all your animosities against the whites, forget the past, and accept the offering of peace which I bring you."

Sitting Bull replied that he hoped that "quiet will again be restored to our country," but he warned that "those forts filled with white soldiers must be abandoned" and that timber-cutting must be stopped. "I will not have the whites cutting our timber above the rivers, especially the oak. I am particularly fond of the little groves of oak trees. I like to look at them and feel a reverence for them, because they endure the winter storms and the summer heat, and like ourselves they seem to thrive and flourish by them."

He did agree to one important thing: he would

send two of his chiefs, Gall and Bull Owl, to talk with the peace commissioners whom Father de Smet represented.

And Sitting Bull kept his word. Less than two months later the Sioux signed the Treaty of Laramie with the U.S. peace commission.

It was a good peace—if only the whites would keep their word.

Sitting Bull was given much of what he asked. The treaty set aside all the land "north of the North Platte River and east of the summits of the Big Horn Mountains" as the Great Sioux Reservation. Here the Tetons could roam at will through millions of acres unsettled by whites, unoccupied by forts or soldiers, unspoiled by railroads or mining operations. The Black Hills, in which the Great Spirit, Manitou, dwelled, would still be sacred. No whites could enter this territory without the permission of Sitting Bull or his chiefs. The treaty was to stay in effect "as long as the grass grows and the rivers flow"—forever.

It was a great victory for Sitting Bull, greater than any he had won in battle—but would the whites keep their word? Meanwhile Sitting Bull stayed on his guard against them and against his old enemies, the Crows. Much as he wanted peace, he found that hardly a summer passed without fighting.

∧·∧·∧

FIVE

War Against the Trespassers

Not only the whites but other tribes, such as the Crows and the Flatheads, envied the Teton Sioux their broad expanse of hunting lands. Sitting Bull was determined to keep them all out, as had been guaranteed by the Treaty of Laramie.

One day early in the winter of 1869 he was sitting in his lodge talking with his old friend, Circling Hawk. The Hunkpapa hunting party was camped near the mouth of the Powder River because the hunting was best at that time of the year in the Yellowstone valley, and the winter's supply of meat had not been brought in. Soon they would take the meat back to the rest of the tribe on the Grand River.

He and Circling Hawk were talking about reports

from their scouts that Crows had been seen lurking in the Sioux tribal preserve. These Crows had no horses and were hunting on foot. It looked like a hard winter, and they would be desperate.

"We must take out a large war party and chase away the Crows or there will not be enough meat in the villages of the Hunkpapa," Sitting Bull was saying. "In the morning, we will ride out. . . ."

Just then a Sioux boy, who had been out hunting buffalo on foot with another boy, came running into the camp crying and yelling. Sitting Bull ran out of his lodge and asked him what had happened.

"I was out hunting with Little Owl," the boy told his chief, "and we had just killed a buffalo. We were skinning it when thirty Crows came upon us. One of them had a horse, the others were on foot. We started running, because we could not fight off thirty of them without lances. That was the right thing to do, wasn't it, Itanchan?"

"It is never anything but foolish to fight when you do not stand a chance," Sitting Bull said gravely. "Where is Little Owl?"

"He is dead!" the boy wailed. He did not try to hide his grief; only white men did that. "The Crows chased us and we were outrunning them. But the Crow on horseback caught up with Little Owl and killed him. They almost caught me, but I hid in a ravine and then came back here by a round-about way."

Sitting Bull raised his lance and shouted for the warriors to gather.

They must mount their horses and catch the Crows who had killed the boy.

"*Hopo! Hopo!*" Sitting Bull shouted, meaning "Let's go! Let's go!"

It was late in the afternoon, but the hastily formed war party set out across the plain in search of the Crows. With a light snow on the ground, it would not be hard to follow them.

They rode north, following the tracks, toward the Spoon Horn Butte. Just below the butte there was a small stream called Big Dry Creek. It wasn't big, but it was dry. They crossed the creek, still following the Crow footprints in the snow, until they came to a small hill surrounded by huge rocks.

Up there in the rocks the Crows were waiting. They had picked a good place to defend themselves.

Night had fallen by then, and the enemy could not be attacked until morning. So Sitting Bull and his warriors wrapped themselves in their blankets and buffalo robes and slept on the snow-covered ground that night.

Shortly after the cold bluish dawn broke, without

waiting to eat, they began attacking the Crows up on the rocky hill. The enemy was armed with bows, rifles, and lances. It would be hard to get at them.

"That place," said Sitting Bull, "is like a fort. Many of us will be killed, but we cannot let one Crow live after what they did to Little Owl."

His adopted brother, Jumping Bull, was at Sitting Bull's side and eager to prove his courage.

"I am wearing the sash of the Warrior Society," he told Sitting Bull. The sash had been guaranteed by the medicine man to protect its wearer from bullets. "Their guns cannot harm me. I will make the Crows empty their guns firing at me; then we will attack."

Jumping Bull, mounted on his fastest horse, rode around the hill at a gallop, taunting the Crows, calling them cowards and old women for staying behind the rocks, and making them fire their rifles at him. He made the circuit of the hill without being hit.

The moment he came back to Sitting Bull, while the Crows were still reloading, the rest of the band began attacking the Crows in the rocks above them. Many Sioux were killed climbing the hill, but not as many as would have been if Jumping Bull hadn't tricked them into emptying their weapons. Sitting Bull himself was in the lead. A Sioux chief did not merely direct a battle; he led the fighting. Sitting Bull counted coup three times up among the rocks and killed every Crow he could reach.

Within ten minutes the Sioux had fought their way over the rock barrier and killed every one of the thirty Crows.

Fourteen of the Sioux were also killed, including the boy Little Owl. Eighteen others were wounded. Sitting Bull, though he had exposed himself more than any other, miraculously escaped without even a scratch.

A village that lost fourteen men in one battle was badly hurt. For they were not merely fourteen warriors no longer able to defend the village and hunt but they were also fourteen men the others had known from their earliest days. Sitting Bull's party returned to the village on the Grand River in mourning as well as in triumph. One of those killed was his uncle, Looks-for-Home, and when Sitting Bull entered his home village he smeared mud on his face, as a token of mourning, and howled with grief.

The battle at Big Dry Creek should have warned other tribes from poaching on the Sioux hunting grounds, but elsewhere in Indian country hard times had come with the white man. The other tribes didn't have their hunting grounds guaranteed by treaty, as Sitting Bull had insisted upon before he agreed to stop fighting the white man.

Thus in Idaho and Montana gold miners were moving in, and killing off the Indians' game. The white men weren't so numerous but they were wasteful hunters. They would kill a buffalo just to eat its liver, or possibly its hump, and then leave the rest to rot in the sun—a ton of meat wasted, which the Indians would have used down to the hoofs and tail. The Indians did not believe in killing carelessly. The animals were their friends, and some were even worshipped as part of a creation their gods charged them with preserving. So the Indians killed only enough to keep themselves alive.

Now that the game was disappearing to the north and west of the Sioux tribal preserve, the neighboring tribes began invading it and killing buffalo. Particularly active in this poaching were the Flatheads, a tribe that roamed the Montana Territory with the Nez Perce, a peaceful hunting and fishing tribe that had been driven out of Idaho by the U.S. cavalry to make room for more prospectors.

In the spring following the battle with the Crows, Sitting Bull decided he would have to teach the Flatheads a lesson. He led a large war party of 400 on the expedition. His scouts soon brought back word that the Flatheads were camped on the Musselshell River.

"*Hopo! Hopo!*" cried his chiefs and the other warriors.

"No," said Sitting Bull, his broad face impassive. "Let us be calm. Let us remember the attack on the Crows in the rocks above the Big Dry, and the fourteen dead we left behind us there."

The others were puzzled, because Sitting Bull was usually the first to shout "*Hopo, hopo!*" But he was learning that strategy could save lives, as his adopted brother Jumping Bull had shown in drawing the Crows' fire.

"Why do you hang back?" Circling Hawk asked him.

"Last night," Sitting Bull explained, perhaps inventing the story to suit his purpose, "I was smoking the pipe. In the smoke I saw a battle with the Flatheads. Many of the enemy were killed, and some of the Sioux."

His followers were always impressed with dreams and prophecies. White men might call it superstition, but to the Sioux omens and portents were a part of wisdom and must be heeded.

"I have thought about this," Sitting Bull continued, "and I consider it a warning that we should be cautious. We should not go flying into the camp of the Flatheads. They have scouts. They will be warned of our coming and prepare an ambush for us.

"I say let us turn this around and prepare an ambush for *them*. We will send a picked war party, small in number, of our youngest warriors and fastest horses. They will ride toward the Flatheads as though they were going to attack them. The Flatheads will come swarming at them like wasps. Our young warriors will lead them toward us, straight into our trap."

Early the next morning a score of the younger braves, led by Sitting Bull's nephew, White Bull, headed out for the Flathead camp. Meanwhile Sitting Bull and the others moved to a patch of brush and young cottonwoods about two miles away.

The younger Sioux rode over the prairie like the wind, until they were in sight of the Flathead village of about 100 tepees. It was just about dawn. One of the Flatheads was outside the village, driving a pony herd out on the prairie. When he saw the Sioux heading toward him, he turned and fled for the camp, shouting the alarm that they were about to be attacked.

In a few moments the Flathead warriors, 100 strong and most of them armed with rifles or pistols, came tearing out of their camp. The Sioux pretended to be surprised at this display of force, paused, then started making a run for it. A hot pursuit followed. Occasionally the young Sioux would halt and make it look as though they were going to stand and fight. Then they would continue their flight. Last of all rode White Bull, who was determined to live up to his uncle's reputation for courage.

When they got close to the brush and trees that screened Sitting Bull and the rest of the war party, White Bull jumped off his horse and challenged the Flathead who was leading the pursuit. The Flathead also dismounted. He approached White Bull carrying a rifle. White Bull was armed only with a lance. The Flathead fired, and his bullet broke White Bull's lance. White Bull then charged at the Flathead and struck him with his broken lance. After counting coup on the fallen Flathead, he dashed into the brush with the others.

Just as the main body of the 100 Flathead warriors came up to the wooded patch, Sitting Bull and the others charged out. The air was filled with shouts, screams, and war whoops. The Flatheads were taken completely by surprise and were heavily outnumbered, but they fought back bravely. Many were killed in the shock of that first charge.

Sitting Bull was in the thick of the fight, as always,

and his fighting blood was running hot. He and six other Sioux chased the Flatheads back to their village. It was a rash thing to do, as Sitting Bull later realized, but he wanted to give the Flatheads a lesson they wouldn't soon forget and discourage them from ever returning to the Sioux hunting grounds.

As they approached the Flathead village, one of the enemy warriors jumped off his horse, armed only with a bow and arrows, and challenged Sitting Bull to fight it out man to man. Sitting Bull immediately accepted the challenge. He was just about to dismount when the Flathead drew back his bowstring and sent an arrow winging its way toward Sitting Bull. The arrow struck him in the right forearm.

He wheeled his horse away from the enemy just as the Flathead let fly with another arrow, which narrowly missed him. He and his six companions rode out of range; then the head of the arrow imbedded in Sitting Bull's forearm was cut off and the shaft pulled out of his wound. He lost so much blood that he fell unconscious and had to be carried back to his own camp.

His wound healed slowly, but Sitting Bull remained at the head of his warriors. For the next two years the Sioux were almost continually on the move, fighting skirmishes with the Crows, who were constantly invading Sioux lands and killing buffalo.

[67]

Meanwhile, Sitting Bull was also forced to keep a suspicious eye on the activities of the white man. The Northern Pacific Railroad was being pushed steadily westward, and from the direction it was taking it appeared that it would invade the Sioux preserves in violation of the Treaty of Laramie. At the same time Grandfather was asking Sitting Bull to come to another "peace" conference at Fort Peck in August, 1872. Peace? They already had peace, didn't they? The summons could only mean that Grandfather wanted the Sioux to give up something.

In the middle of August a surveying party for the railroad reached the Yellowstone River. It traveled under a heavy escort of cavalry. Sitting Bull and his warriors were camped on the Powder River a few miles away and were watching every move the whites made.

The surveyors, guarded by the soldiers, were working their way along the south bank of the Yellowstone. Sitting Bull knew that meant the railroad would run there, in violation of the treaty stating that no tracks would be laid across any part of the land guaranteed to the Sioux. And yet the whites expected him to come to Fort Peck and talk about "peace" only a week from then.

His warriors were eager to attack the whites and chase them off Sioux land, but Sitting Bull said it might all be a mistake. They must talk to the soldiers and surveyors first and warn them that they were trespassing on the Sioux reservation.

"The only talk the whites understand is from rifles," protested Crazy Horse, who was gaining renown as a warrior second only to Sitting Bull. He was now the chief's second-in-command.

"No, there'll be no fighting before we talk," Sitting Bull said. "We will tell them they have no right to be on the Yellowstone."

He and his warriors rode toward the whites' camp on Arrow Creek in the Yellowstone valley. Crazy Horse, White Bull, and Circling Hawk were among those with Sitting Bull.

It was shortly past dawn when they approached the camp. There was no chance for talk. A sentinel gave the alarm in the whites' camp, and the soldiers took up their positions behind the bank of the creek. One of Sitting Bull's braves was killed and many were wounded in that first fusillade, fired without warning, without waiting to see whether the Sioux intentions were friendly or not.

The fighting went on all morning—an exchange of rifle fire between the soldiers behind the bank and the Sioux out on the prairie. Sitting Bull knew he couldn't afford to charge the whites, and the cavalry couldn't be taunted into coming out in the open.

This kind of fighting bored and irked Sitting Bull. He was a man of action. Squaws could do the kind of fighting the white man seemed to prefer. To show his contempt he suddenly rose and walked calmly out on the prairie between the white soldiers and his own followers. He was armed only with his long pipe. When he was about 100 yards from his own line, he sat down, took out flint and steel, and struck a light for his pipe. For a few moments he sat there calmly puffing the pipe. Both the whites and the Indians, equally astonished at his bold gesture, stopped firing.

"Any Indians who wish to have a smoke," he called to his followers, "come out here and join me."

His nephew, White Bull, and his old friend, Circling Hawk, were among the first to take Sitting Bull's dare and squat near him. The pipe passed from hand to hand. When it was finished, they all rose from their haunches and unhurriedly strolled back to their own line.

As a final gesture of contempt, he and his party jumped on their horses and rode along the creek,

Sitting Bull and his nephew White Bull

only a few yards from the line of white riflemen, and then back to their own camp.

During the rest of the summer, Sitting Bull skirmished constantly with the cavalry escorting the survey party. Even then, with Grandfather in Washington breaking his promises, Sitting Bull held back from declaring an all-out war. He merely wanted to discourage the whites from entering the Yellowstone valley with their railroad and the settlers it would bring.

But he told his people, regarding the whites, "If they come shooting, shoot back."

There was no more talk of peace at Fort Peck or anywhere else.

SIX.

The Coming of Custer

Despite Broken promises, treaty violations, and other provocations, Sitting Bull kept the peace for the next two years.

"In the end," he told Crazy Horse and other leading chiefs of the Teton Sioux, "there will be a big battle. The whites will keep coming, and we will have to resist. But I want to live in peace as long as possible. The whites have many men and many guns, and they never stop coming. They are a force like the wind. How do you resist the wind?"

Once he and a hunting party came across a gaunt and starving white man wandering across the prairie. The man had been eating the bark off trees. He wore the tattered blue uniform, with a yellow stripe down the leg, of the U.S. cavalry.

The men with Sitting Bull suggested that the white man be killed.

Sitting Bull looked on the white man, lying half-dead in the grass, with pity.

"No," he said after thinking about it. "He is wearing the blue coat. That means he has deserted the white man's army. He is no longer our enemy. He has no gun, no horse, and he is being hunted by the white soldiers. He is the enemy of our enemy, which makes him our friend. He is leaving our country, so he should go in peace."

Sitting Bull fed the deserter and sent him on his way.

During that time of waiting, he also made peace with the Assiniboine, who were willing to stop fighting with the Sioux largely because they had heard of how Sitting Bull had adopted their tribesman, Jumping Bull, as his brother. Thus the Assiniboine allowed him, along with a small war party, to go through their territory on an expedition to the Canadian border. Some Canadian Indians had been raiding Sitting Bull's horse herds, and he wanted to teach them a lesson. On his way back from the border, Sitting Bull's war party, less than a score of braves, was attacked by a band of strange Indians from ambush. Sitting Bull was badly outnumbered, and it looked as though he and all his warriors might be killed, when suddenly a war party of Assiniboine rode up and drove off the Indians attacking Sitting Bull. His life was saved largely because many years before he had taken mercy on the Assiniboine boy, who was now one of his bravest warriors.

When he returned from that narrow scrape, he learned that Grandfather was again stepping boldly toward the Sioux preserves. The whites were sending a column of cavalry into the Black Hills, in southwestern South Dakota, the dwelling place of the Great Spirit!

Sitting Bull was told by messengers from the army that the white cavalry, under a colonel named George A. Custer, were just going up into the Badlands, as the whites called the Black Hills, to look around.

"The Black Hills belong to me," Sitting Bull told the army messengers. "If the whites try to take them, I will fight."

He did not interfere with Custer's column as it invaded the eastern part of the Sioux reserve. If the soldiers only looked around and then withdrew, it was all right—certainly not worth fighting a war about. He was willing to take Grandfather's word that they would not do anything else.

What Sitting Bull didn't know was that Custer's column had several other purposes besides sightseeing. One reason for the expedition was to select a site for a military post in the Black Hills. The expedition also knew that for years rumors had been floating around that there were rich veins of gold in the Sioux preserves. So along with the soldiers rode a geologist and two gold miners. Once again Grandfather was breaking his word.

The Custer expedition withdrew after making its surveys, and as far as Sitting Bull knew, the Black Hills were still sacred to the Great Manitou. Among the whites, however, the word quickly got around that the miners with Custer had found considerable gold in French Creek and there might be "a belt of gold territory 30 miles wide" in the Badlands of Dakota Territory.

The reports of heavy gold deposits in the Black Hills sped around the settlements and cities of the West. Prospectors who tried to invade the Sioux lands, however, were at first turned away by the cavalry. The U.S. government wanted to make a deal with Sitting Bull before he realized how much the Badlands were worth to the whites. Government officials refused to believe that the Indians would be as unwilling to sell their sacred hills as the whites would be unwilling to sell their own hope of heaven. Even then, white adventurers by the hundred were gathering in Cheyenne, Wyoming Territory, and waiting for the gold rush to begin the moment the U.S. cavalry let down the bars.

A treaty commission was sent out from Washington early in 1875 to offer the Sioux $6,000,000 for the Black Hills part of their reservation. Sitting Bull and the other leading chiefs indignantly turned the offer down. How could they sell the place where their god, the Great Manitou, lived?

The treaty commissioners refused to listen to the Sioux claims that they could never sell the Black Hills without selling their own souls.

When they returned to Washington, the army took over. It sent a message to Sitting Bull ordering him, at his camp on the Powder River, to come to the Standing Rock Agency in Dakota Territory, with all his people. It had been a terribly hard winter, but Sitting Bull refused to be lured to the "protection" of the white soldiers even by the promise of plenty of rations and warm clothing for his people.

He was enraged when he learned that the U.S. cavalry was now allowing hundreds of gold miners to rush into the Black Hills and that a large force under General George Crook had been sent from Fort Fetterman to round up the Sioux and their allies, the Cheyenne, and put them on reservations by force, if necessary. The white soldiers would come

Gen. Crook and troopers

shooting this time. Either the Sioux and the other "free" tribes would allow themselves to be penned up, treated like children (if they behaved) or like outlaws (if they refused to settle down to farming as a way of life), or they would be killed. No excuse was made to Sitting Bull by Grandfather for breaking the government's solemn promises and guarantees. There was gold—hundreds of millions worth —on Sioux lands, and the whites meant to have it.

For eight years, since he had talked with "Black Robe," Father de Smet, Sitting Bull had kept the peace and had fired on white soldiers only when they attacked him. Now he was fighting mad. A council of elders and chiefs was held on the Tongue River, at which Sitting Bull proclaimed:

"We are an island of Indians in a lake of whites. We must stand together, or they will wipe us out separately. The white soldiers have come shooting. They want war. All right, we'll give it to them."

A short time later he sent messengers to all the fighting and hunting tribes west of the Missouri—the Arapaho, the Cheyenne, and the others who considered themselves free men—to come to a great council and decide how to resist the white invaders. Never before had all the Indians of the Plains fought together against a common enemy. Perhaps they could not be persuaded to forget their old quarrels and past wars, but Sitting Bull saw that they must stand together.

That spring of 1876 bands of Indians from all over the country west of the Missouri began traveling toward the meeting place that Sitting Bull had designated. It was his own camp in the bend of the Rosebud, in the country where he had hunted for many years—the Yellowstone country. From all directions the trails were alive with Indians converging on the Rosebud. There were the various Sioux tribes, and the Cheyenne, the Arapaho, and the Blackfeet. Their tepees, pitched around Sitting Bull's village, stretched for miles. It was the greatest gathering of Indians ever seen on the Great Plains. The nights were filled with the beat of the drums and the thump of warriors' feet dancing around the camp fires.

For many it was like a great outdoor convention, a picnic that lasted for days, a gigantic family reunion. Squaws gossiped, children played, dogs chased each other through the villages.

But for the chiefs of the various tribes it was a life-and-death business, the survival of their people.

At the first council meeting the Cheyenne announced that their chief, Two Moons, would lead them in the coming war against the whites. The question of who would exercise the supreme command of all the Plains Indians was quickly settled. Two Moons rose and said, "It should not take long to decide who will lead us all. There is only one man in all our minds—Sitting Bull. He alone is spoken of in the 200 lodges of the Cheyenne, the six villages of Sioux, and all the others. He must be the war chief of us all."

There was no dispute over that suggestion.

"*Hau! Hau! Hau!*" all the chiefs around the council fire said in agreement.

Sitting Bull rose to speak. He was then forty-three years old, still limping from the old foot wound, his right arm still stiff from the Flathead arrow, and there was gray in his long black hair. There were many other chiefs more impressive looking, taller, straighter, handsomer, but there was an inconquerable light in Sitting Bull's eyes and steadfastness in his broad face. They needed a man who would never quit, no matter what the odds, and Sitting Bull's whole life, from infancy on, testified to his sticking power.

Now that the vote was for war, war against all whites wherever and however they might be found, Sitting Bull told the chiefs they must prepare for long fighting with no quarter given. "Send your young braves out in twos and threes on horse-stealing raids. We will need many horses. Do not send more than four men in each party. The soldiers won't bother to chase such a few men. Collect all the weapons you can find, particularly firearms. Store up food, for we may be on the march for a long time.

"And one more thing: kill every white you find. Tell your young warriors this. If you meet a white man, kill him and take his horse and gun. The whites have shown that they will give us no mercy, no quarter. We have not asked for this war, but we must win now that there is no escape from it, or we will die as a people."

Then Sitting Bull turned to the sun, to which he prayed as to a god. "Protect us and protect the wild game. Let good men on earth have more power. Let my people survive and live as they have always lived. Make us brave in war and worthy of victory."

Sitting Bull then led all the tribes in a Sun Dance that lasted two days and two nights, a form of worship in which hundreds of warriors danced until they dropped. Sitting Bull himself fell unconscious. When he was revived, he announced that he had had a vision, that he had dreamed the Indians would defeat the whites in a great battle.

SEVEN

Sitting Bull's Last Stand

As the June days and nights passed in 1876, it became apparent that a great battle would be fought between the Indians and the whites, the greatest anyone had ever known. Sitting Bull's scouts were riding everywhere, night and day, and coming back to report what they saw.

Three or four separate forces of white soldiers were coming together from different directions, Sitting Bull told his chief lieutenant, the young Sioux chief, Crazy Horse. They would try to trap the Indians in the middle.

"If we let this happen, if we are caught in the trap," Sitting Bull said, "we will not have a chance. They have too many soldiers and too many guns."

"We can outfight them," Crazy Horse said. His

spirit was much like Sitting Bull's in his youth. But Sitting Bull had learned with the years that fighting spirit was not enough. The whites were so numerous that you had to outthink them as well as outfight them.

"No," he said, "the whites are brave, too. They know how to fight together." Sitting Bull held up his scarred warrior's hand. "They are like this. One finger, see? It is nothing. But five fingers together—they make a fist."

"We can't keep the tribes together much longer without a fight," Crazy Horse told his leader. "They are getting restless. There isn't enough grass to feed all the horses."

"Then we will move from the valley of the Rosebud to the valley of the Little Big Horn tomorrow," Sitting Bull said. "But we must stay together. If we separate, we will be beaten one by one. Remember the fingers and the fist. One tribe separated from the others is nothing. Together we can strike each column of whites as it comes up against us."

Several days after the Indians moved their huge camp—thousands of tepees, thousands of people, thousands of horses—to the valley of the Little Big Horn, Sitting Bull learned from his scouts that one column of white soldiers had arrived in the area. It was commanded by the famous Indian-fighter General Crook and was made up of more than 1,000 soldiers with 250 Indian scouts. Many of the Crows had joined the white man's army and most had gone to reservations, which only made the Sioux hate them more.

General Crook's column moved into the valley of the Rosebud, which the Indians had just vacated. Sitting Bull sent Crazy Horse with 1,000 warriors from all the tribes to meet Crook and drive him away. Then, suddenly, he decided to go himself. He couldn't bear sitting in his tepee and waiting to hear news of the battle. He gathered up his Hunkpapa guard—Jumping Bull, Circling Hawk, his nephew White Bull, and all the others—and rode furiously for the valley of the Rosebud. He arrived just in time to join the attack on Crook. All day long Sitting Bull and Crazy Horse with their Sioux and Cheyenne warriors attacked the white soldiers, and by sundown Crook was so badly beaten that he could only retreat. It was a fine victory. But it almost ruined Sitting Bull's plan.

"We've beaten the whites!" his warriors cried. "Now they will leave us in peace and we can go hunting."

All night Sitting Bull argued before the chiefs and elders at the council fire.

"We must stay together," he pleaded. "The

whites are not beaten; only a small part of their army is. This is the lesson I have learned from fighting the whites: they always keep coming at you. You can win ten victories and count 1,000 coups and take 10,000 scalps, but they are not discouraged. Their cities are full of people and they raise new armies. We have beaten only one force. In a few days, two or three others will arrive to fight as Crook did. If we separate, if our hunting bands go out for fresh meat, we will be beaten separately. Stay together. It will not be long."

All night he argued against that spirit of restlessness that had always possessed the Indians. They simply couldn't stay in one place for more than a few days. They could not think of the day after tomorrow. Perhaps the greatest victory of his life was won by Sitting Bull that night, when he persuaded the various tribes, whom he could lead but not command, that they must stay in camp there on the Little Big Horn and wait *together* for the rest of the white forces.

"Remember," he said, "that I had a vision of a great victory. That is still to come. Men will sing of our deeds around the campfires of the Sioux and Cheyenne and Blackfeet and Arapaho until the end of time—or they will remember us as fools, who let themselves and those who came after them be made slaves and children of the whites without a fight."

The chiefs were persuaded to stay a while longer in the valley of the Little Big Horn, at least as long as there were enough buffalo and other game to feed their people.

Days went by. The hunters ranged farther and farther in search of game, and nights passed in dancing around the camp fires.

How long, Sitting Bull wondered, could he hold the tribes together here in the valley of the Little Big Horn? Why didn't the other columns of white soldiers arrive?

He spoke of his worries on the night of June 24. That same night Colonel George Custer, the man who had invaded the sacred Black Hills, spoke to his officers, not many miles away from the great Indian camp, of how much he wanted to beat the Indians. Custer was supposed to wait for other columns; he had been ordered not to attack by himself, because he might be beaten as General Crook was. But Custer was hungry for fame, he craved glory, and he believed that if he alone, with his famous regiment, the Seventh Cavalry, could defeat Sitting Bull, he would be picked to run for President of the United States. For George Custer, the road to the White House lay through the valley of the Little Big Horn. He could not wait because that meant he would have to

Gen. Custer, June 25, 1876

share the glory. The next day, he told the officers of the Seventh Cavalry they would attack and win the greatest victory of the Indian wars. And the name of Custer would be forever glorious.

June 25, 1876, was a clear warm day. There was little wind, and the dust barely stirred on the trails. The women in the Indian villages along the Little Big Horn were working at their daily tasks. Many of the boys too young to be warriors were out fishing.

Sitting Bull was sitting in the big lodge where the war councils were held, thinking over his problems. His greatest worry was not the white soldiers converging on him in three columns, from north, south, and east, but the impatience of his own people. It was early summer and the hunting parties were eager to take off. There was little hunting around an area occupied by thousands of Indians, with more thousands of whites just over the horizon. All the game had been driven away. There had to be a fight soon or all the people he had gathered together for the last stand of the Plains Indians would simply melt away.

A brave named Fat Bear interrupted his meditations. He had a report that scouts had spotted white troops moving up to the Little Big Horn. They were on both sides, north and south, of the huge Indian encampment. A short time ago two Hunkpapa boys out looking for stray horses had been fired upon and pursued by white troopers.

"Then they're coming!" Sitting Bull said, jumping up. The light of battle flared in his eyes. "The waiting is over. Good. It is always the same with the whites. They stick close together. When you see a few of them out on patrol or scouting, it means the others are not far behind. Sound the alarm, Fat Bear!"

In a moment the villages were alive with warriors rushing to collect their weapons, running for their horses, and riding off in bands of whooping horsemen.

Sitting Bull's two nephews, White Bull and One Bull, whom he regarded almost as sons, came running up to him. They were buckling on their cartridge belts. One of them handed Sitting Bull a war club with a stone wrapped to its head, which he now always carried in the forefront of battle.

"Now we go to fight," White Bull told him.

"Go ahead," Sitting Bull said. "Fear nothing. Go straight in. Find the white soldiers and kill them all."

As he hurried off to mount his own war horse, he could hear the sounds of battle beginning.

The Indians were camped on the south bank of the

Little Big Horn, which runs east and west. Custer's Seventh Cavalry was coming toward them from the east. As soon as he learned there were Indian villages along the river, he unwisely divided up his command to attack them. He thought they contained a few hundred warriors, instead of thousands. So he took one squadron with him to attack the north end of the sprawling Indian encampment, while Major Reno led another squadron against the village on the southern side. The rest of the regiment was assigned to guard its wagon trains and supplies.

Sitting Bull and a band of his Hunkpapa warriors rode to the south, where the sounds of firing were heaviest at the moment.

They struck Major Reno's command just north of a stand of timber and swarmed all over the white cavalrymen. The whites saw that they were outnumbered and would have to fight for their lives, so they dismounted and fled back to a line of trees, where they could fire from behind fallen logs.

"Work around them," Sitting Bull shouted to his braves. "Don't let them get away."

He ordered his old friend, Circling Hawk, to lead the attack on the whites in the timber. Once he would have led that attack himself but now he was, in effect, a general. He had to think as well as fight.

[91]

It seemed to him that the whites must be playing a trick on him. They couldn't be so stupid as to attack his villages with only a few hundred men. That meant another attack would be launched at him from another direction. He must keep his forces between the camp and the enemy.

He saw that the whites in the timber were being driven back and that many were running for their horses so they could get away alive. Many whites had already been killed. Sitting Bull rode after his braves, catching up with one band led by his nephew One Bull, who was starting after the fleeing whites.

"Let them go," Sitting Bull ordered One Bull. "Let them live to tell the truth about this battle."

By "truth" he meant that the whites had attacked him, though they always claimed they had been attacked by the Indians. His villages had been peaceful that morning. They had not carried the fight to the whites. The whites, without warning, had come shooting and killing. Sitting Bull was looking ahead to the days and years when the battle would be only a memory, and he wanted the record clear on one thing—the white man had started the fighting. The whites would call it "Custer's Last Stand." It would be more accurate to say it was "Sitting Bull's Last Stand."

He ordered White Bull and all the others to return

[92]

to the villages and protect the women and children.

Sitting Bull himself, with a few followers, rode north where another force of Indian warriors led by Crazy Horse and other chiefs were watching for trouble from that direction. It was good that they had been placed there. He rode through the camps the Indians had abandoned days before in search of better grass.

Sitting Bull arrived just as five companies of white cavalry under Custer himself began attacking from the north, unaware that they were going up against the massed forces of all the fighting Indians still hostile to the idea of living on government rations. It wasn't until after the battle that Sitting Bull even knew he was fighting the Seventh Cavalry or that it was led by Custer, whom he called "Long Hair" (and sometimes "Squaw Killer") because the white commander had worn his golden hair shoulder length until shortly before the battle. He hated Custer because the colonel had commanded the expedition two years before into the Black Hills.

In any case, Custer and his five companies didn't stand a chance. Before they knew what was happening, they were surrounded by thousands of screaming, whooping warriors led by Crazy Horse and Sitting Bull. It was all over in less than an hour. Every single one of the white soldiers was killed.

Yet to Sitting Bull the battle itself was a minor one. He had fought many hard battles against both whites and Indians. This one was so easy because the white men had been so stupid. They had attacked a force that outnumbered them more than ten to one. Not only that, they had divided up and attacked the Indians separately. The most ignorant war chief in the Indian nations would not have behaved so foolishly.

But still it was a great victory. Sitting Bull knew

before the day was over that he had handed the whites a defeat such as they had never suffered before.

Sitting Bull merely asked his chiefs, after the firing ended, "Are they all killed?"

"Yes," he was told.

"Then let's go back to camp."

He rode back to the Hunkpapa village with his warriors, but he could not prevent other bands from staying behind on the battlefield and looting the possessions of the dead white soldiers. He tried to stop them, but the Indian custom was to loot, and the warriors could not understand his reasoning that such a practice would be held against them in the future. The whites would keep coming at him, he knew that, and it would be harder to arrange a peace if they felt bitterly against him.

And taking the white man's goods was bad in another way. "Because you have taken the spoils," he said, "you will be spoiled yourselves. You will want the white man's goods, and you will sell yourselves to get them. He will have you at his mercy. In time you will starve at his hands."

By nightfall his warning was borne out. Many of the warriors of other bands took the whiskey the white soldiers carried in their canteens and got violently drunk.

Sitting Bull himself refused to drink and wouldn't allow any of the Hunkpapa to share the whiskey. It was proper to mourn for the dead, and the Hunkpapa did so even while the Indians in the other villages were drunkenly firing their guns at the stars. Sitting Bull told his people to mourn not only for their own dead but "for those brave white men who are lying up there on the hillside."

The next morning Sitting Bull's scouts brought him word that the white soldiers driven away from the south end of the Indian encampment the day before had taken up positions on a bluff several miles to the east. Sitting Bull tried to think like a white general. Did that mean they were holding a position that could be reinforced by other troops coming from the east, or by Crook from the south? If so, they would be like a thorn in his side.

He decided to attack the whites on the bluff and rode out with most of the braves who were not suffering from drunkenness. They had plenty of ammunition now, almost 10,000 rounds seized from the whites the day before. His own instincts told him there had been enough killing, but his followers were eager to follow up their victory.

All that morning his warriors, dismounted, charged the white soldiers on the bluff.

Many were killed and wounded on both sides as

[97]

they fought on the steep wooded slope under a broiling late-June sun.

Finally Sitting Bull decided it was useless to go on attacking. The whites had been whipped, and enough was enough.

"Let them go," he told his war chiefs. "They came into our country, they attacked our villages, and now many are dead. It is enough. If we kill them all, they will only send a bigger army against us."

The Indians withdrew, and the rest of the Seventh Cavalry was spared.

That night there was a great victory dance in the Indian encampment. Sitting Bull, however, did not dance. He stared into the flames of the camp fire. There was more to think about than dead enemies and captured supplies. What was to come after victory?

"I think," he told Circling Hawk, "we are in for a time of great trouble."

∴∴∴

EIGHT

The Long Retreat to Grandmother

SITTING BULL's brooding at the moment of victory was well justified.   Almost as soon as the big
camp on the Little Big Horn broke up, he learned
that the whites were redoubling their efforts to wipe
him out with all his followers if they did not surrender and submit to living under the guns of a white
cavalry fort.   General John Gibbon was coming
down from the north with one force, General Crook
was coming back after his initial defeat, and General
Alfred H. Terry was advancing from the east.

He still had the Sioux around him, but it looked
as though they, too, would break up and go their
separate ways.

Calling a tribal council, he told Crazy Horse and
the other leading Sioux chiefs that the victory—what

[99]

the whites called the Battle of the Little Big Horn —had called down many additional dangers on their heads. The wisest thing, he said, was to withdraw before they were trapped by the converging columns of white soldiers.

"Run away from the whites after we have beaten them?" Crazy Horse demanded fiercely. He had won great prestige among the Sioux for his leadership; it was now almost equal to Sitting Bull's, and he knew it and was willing to use it.

"It is better than staying and being killed," Sitting Bull said calmly. "We must think of the women and the children. Now that we have beaten the whites so badly, they will never let us rest. Our land is small and getting smaller. It is an island in a lake of white faces. We have two ways to go if we want peace. We can go to the land of the Spaniards [Mexico] or to the land of the Grandmother [Canada]."

Mexico was far off, a hot country unlike the northern plains, and none of the Sioux had ever been there. However, Sitting Bull knew that the Santee branch of his tribe had fled to Canada during the Civil War, after massacring hundreds of white settlers at New Ulm, Minnesota. Canada was much like Sioux country—hot in the summer, cold in the winter.

"We can find peace in the land of the Grandmother," Sitting Bull argued before the tribal council. "I do not understand why the Redcoats gave us and our land to the Americans. We are the Grandmother's children."

By that Sitting Bull meant that he considered the Sioux British citizens rather than American, because originally the British had owned all of America except for small areas claimed by the French and Spanish.

In spite of all his arguments, Crazy Horse and his band of 300 warriors rode off into the mountains. They should have listened to Sitting Bull. The next spring Crazy Horse and many of his followers surrendered at Camp Robinson, Nebraska, lured in by the whites' promise that Crazy Horse would be made supreme chief of all the Sioux in place of Sitting Bull. When Crazy Horse learned he had been tricked into surrendering, he went wild with rage. One of the white soldiers stabbed him in the back and killed him.

By the fall of 1876 Sitting Bull and his people were camped near the Slim Buttes above the Grand River. Nearby were a band of the Minniconjou tribe of Sioux.

One morning in September Sitting Bull was in his tepee preparing to go out on the hunt. His people had been on the move all that summer, but they had managed to gather a good supply of game, berries, and fruit, all of which were sun-dried for the winter.

A man from the Minniconjou came running up crying that his village was being attacked by white soldiers.

It was General Crook's column, as Sitting Bull soon learned, which had caught up with him and was hungry for revenge for the defeat he had inflicted several months before.

Sitting Bull jumped on his white war horse, gathered up his warriors, and rode like the wind for the Minniconjou village. They found the white soldiers killing women and children as well as Minniconjou warriors.

They charged and drove the whites out of the village and across a nearby creek. Then the whites dismounted and took cover. With their better guns they were able to kill many of the attacking Sioux. Sitting Bull kept charging for hours but the firing line set up by General Crook would not break. He also learned that his 500 warriors were greatly outnumbered by the whites. So he wisely withdrew. That way he could haul off his wounded and bury his dead.

General Crook sent him a message ordering him to

surrender unconditionally, but Sitting Bull refused. He and his people would fight if they could, run if they must. So they moved westward, into the Yellowstone country. There he found that the U.S. army was sending in troops and wagon trains with materials for building a fort at the mouth of the Tongue River. Once again the whites were breakings their agreement.

Sitting Bull sent a message to General Nelson A. Miles, who had just come north after defeating and rounding up the tribes of the Southern Plains to take charge of the operations against the Sioux, Cheyenne, Nez Perce, and other tribes who refused to live off the white man's bounty. It warned him:

"I want to know what you are doing on this road. You scare all the buffalo away. I want to hunt in this place. I want you to turn back from here. . . ."

A few weeks later General Miles, whom Sitting Bull called "Bear Coat," came to parley with Sitting Bull. They both talked of peace, but Sitting Bull wouldn't discuss surrender. If "Bear Coat" would give him ammunition, he would continue hunting peacefully and not interfere with the white soldiers. General Miles agreed.

When Sitting Bull went back for another meeting with General Miles, however, he found that the general had placed a Gatling gun—which was an early type of machine gun—in position so that it was aimed at Sitting Bull and his companions. He flew into a rage and said the peace talks were off. He would not talk peace when the enemy threatened him with force.

It was late in the year, no time to be traveling, but Sitting Bull and his people packed up their tepees and winter food supply and set out for the Canadian border, "Grandmother's country," where they believed they would be safe.

They moved slowly and deliberately, once stopping to fight off a company of white cavalry that had been dogging their trail.

Finally, with great rejoicing they crossed the border. The Royal Mounted Police who were waiting for them would treat them justly and fairly. Sitting Bull immediately let the Mounties know that he wanted only to live in peace. He also went around to all the neighboring tribes of Canadian Indians and assured them of the same thing.

To prevent his young braves from following the old custom of going out on the warpath to prove their manhood, he organized a group called "Sitting Bull's Soldiers," who would act as his police. If a Sioux stole or did something else against the Cana-

Gen. Miles and the Gatling Gun

dian law, Sitting Bull punished the crime at the request of the Mounted Police. He had no trouble with either the Mounties or the other Indian tribes in Canada.

All was well with Grandmother. It was Grandfather, the United States government, which kept bothering him.

Word reached Sitting Bull that the Sioux who stayed on the other side of the boundary had been forced to sign a new treaty with the U.S. government, by which the Black Hills and most of the former Great Sioux Reservation were handed over to the whites. All Sioux had to go to the Standing Rock Agency in Dakota Territory, where they were given food and clothing. Any who refused were treated as outlaws, hunted down, and killed.

Grandfather had taken everything from the Indians—their lands, their game, their Great Manitou—and now he wanted the last thing they had left, their freedom.

Sitting Bull swore he would never willingly go back to that. The U.S. government kept sending him messages asking him to return with his people. Scouts and missionaries visited him and said he was an American citizen, whether he liked it or not, and must come back. Among those who visited Sitting Bull and his people in their Canadian exile was a newspaper correspondent named John Finerty, who wrote:

"An Indian mounted on a cream-colored pony, and holding in his hand an eagle's wing which did duty as a fan, spurred in back of the chiefs and stared stolidly at me. His hair, parted in the ordinary Sioux fashion, was without a plume. His broad face, with a prominent hooked nose and wide jaws, was destitute of paint. His fierce, half-bloodshot eyes gleamed from under brows which displayed large perceptive organs, and, as he sat there on his horse, regarding me with a look which seemed blended of curiosity and insolence, I did not need to be told that he was Sitting Bull. After a little, the savage dismounted . . . he limped slightly as though from an old wound. He sat upon the ground, and was soon engirdled by a crowd of young warriors with whom he was an especial favorite, representing the unquenchable hostility of the aboriginal savage to the hated Palefaces."

Sitting Bull and his people might have lived out their days in peace on the Canadian side of the border, but for one thing: the United States and Canada had a treaty by which each government was supposed to return any Indians who strayed across the border. Both governments were working against Sitting Bull's plan for a peaceful exile in Canada.

Canada was insisting that the United States take the Sioux back, and the American government wanted them back, perhaps because the army feared Sitting Bull would raid across the border and use Canada as a sanctuary where he couldn't be attacked in retaliation.

Sitting Bull had in thing in his favor: he knew the Canadians wouldn't want to force him to return or bring on a battle between the Sioux and the Mounted Police. That meant Sitting Bull could play for time. He was a great diplomat, and he knew how to stretch out negotiations endlessly; he had more patience, in that sort of thing, than the white men, who wanted to get the job over and done with. Palaver, as the Indians called it—Sitting Bull was good at that. He talked endlessly to Canadian commissioners and American commissioners.

If talk would keep his people from being sent into American captivity, he would palaver until the stars fell from the heavens. His determination to keep stalling was only strengthened when in 1878 General Miles chased Chief Joseph and his Nez Perce Indians for hundreds of miles and finally trapped most of them in the Bear Paw Mountains. About 100 Nez Perce escaped from the trap and fled across the border to join Sitting Bull and his people. He was greatly affected by the stories told him by the Nez

Perce of the merciless way in which they had been hounded by the whites.

Nevertheless, he could not refuse to meet with the U.S. Peace Commission, headed by General Terry, which came to Canada late in 1878. General Terry promised a "full pardon" to all who surrendered and food and shelter at the Standing Rock Agency, and he seemed to believe he was being generous in offering such terms. That Indians should value their freedom and their own way of life was, apparently, beyond the understanding of any white man. So Terry was surprised when Sitting Bull replied in anger:

"For sixty-four years you have kept me and my people on the run and treated us bad. We could go nowhere else, so we took refuge here. Look at me. I have ears, I have eyes to see with. If you think me a fool, you are a bigger fool than I am. You come here to tell us lies, but we do not want to listen to them. Go back home where you came from. . . ."

He refused to consider returning to the United States, and for two more years negotiations dragged on between him, the Canadian government, and U.S. officials. Sitting Bull was playing for time, and he did it skillfully, but in the end he was forced to leave Canada with his people.

They crossed the border after five peaceful years on Canadian soil and were promptly disarmed by the American troops who met them.

Sitting Bull himself surrendered with all the undiminished pride of a great Sioux chief.

"Let it be recorded," he said, "that I am the last of my people to lay down my gun."

Then, herded like sheep by the cavalry, they were all escorted to the Standing Rock Agency, where they would live under the guns at Fort Yates.

ᐱ·ᐱ·ᐱ

NINE

Touring with Buffalo Bill Cody

WHEN SITTING BULL and his people returned to Dakota territory against their will, they found that both the Indian Bureau, the government agency in charge of them, and the U.S. army deeply resented them. They were received as prisoners, rather than as wards of the government. The man in charge of the Indian Agency at Standing Rock was Major James McLaughlin, an honest but limited man, who feared Sitting Bull's influence over the Sioux and believed that the chief was plotting another uprising.

Sitting Bull also found that other Sioux, who had surrendered earlier, resented him for having the courage to lead the Hunkpapa to Canada. Two rival chiefs, Gall and John Grass, had established them-

John Grass and Gall

selves on the reservation at Standing Rock. With Major McLaughlin's encouragement they claimed to be the real leaders of the Sioux Nation. The army and the Indian Bureau spread the word that Sitting Bull wasn't really a great war chief but only a medicine man. Sitting Bull was a medicine man but he was, above all, a great leader.

Many of the younger Sioux were persuaded to join the Indian Police, under the command of white officers, which maintained order on the reservation. All Indians who listened to the Indian Bureau, the army, the missionaries, and traders—all the whites at Fort Yates—were given special privileges.

Meanwhile, Sitting Bull and his Hunkpapa were forced to live in huts more or less like white men and give up their hunting and roving. They were supposed to become farmers, but Washington did not live up to its promises to give them the means to till the land. They couldn't do it with their bare hands. They couldn't raise sheep and cattle without breeding stock. All they got was barely enough food and clothing to keep them from starving or freezing to death.

A Congressional committee came out to investigate conditions at Standing Rock, and Sitting Bull spoke bluntly to them: "It is your own doing that I am here. You sent me here and told me to live as you do, and it is not right for me to live in poverty.

"I asked the Grandfather for hogs and sheep to raise stock from. I want some agricultural implements so that I will not have to work bare-handed.

"I want to tell you that our rations have been reduced to almost nothing, and many of the people have starved to death. Now I beg you to have the amount of our rations increased so our children will not starve. I want clothing too. Look at the men around here and see how poorly they are dressed."

And all that Sitting Bull got in reply was a speech by a senator from Illinois, who declared that the Sioux should be grateful for the handouts they were given. They were living on government charity and should keep their mouths shut. No mention was made of the fact that millions of acres of tribal lands had simply been seized by the government or that hundreds of millions of dollars worth of gold was being taken out of the Black Hills, from which the Indians received nothing but broken promises.

Sitting Bull and his people kept the peace and tried to scratch out a living on their corn patches above the Grand River. The chief himself was in his fifties now, which was old for an Indian who had spent so many years on the warpath, but his spirit was still strong and defiant. Shortly before the battle of the Little Big Horn he had married again.

His wife was a slim and comely young woman named Running Deer, and she had given him a son, Crowfoot, who was then eleven years old. But he chafed in captivity. His mood was expressed in a little poem he wrote:

"A warrior
I have been.
Now
It is all over.
A hard time
I have."

One night in the summer of 1884, three years after he had returned to Standing Rock, he was talking with his old friend, Circling Hawk. The old days were constantly in his mind. "On a night like this, when we were free, we would be dancing," he recalled. "For miles around there would be nothing but silence. We would sleep in our tepees, knowing that the next day, like all others, would be spent on the hunt. There were no white men to tell us what to do, to pity us, or to hand us sacks of flour and pieces of half-rotten beef if we behave ourselves."

"What can we do?" Circling Hawk asked, passing the pipe to Sitting Bull.

"Nothing. We are caught in a trap. We cannot

even leave this little piece of land unless the Indian Bureau lets us."

"We could run away."

"No," said Sitting Bull after thinking it over. "The whites are too strong. They and their forts are everywhere. There is no place to run."

The next year, much to his surprise, Sitting Bull was offered a job off the reservation.

It happened one day in the spring of 1885, when a tall, courtly man with white hair and a kindly manner came to Standing Rock to talk to him. His name was Colonel William F. Cody, better known as Buffalo Bill. In the old days Buffalo Bill had been a cavalry scout and later he had operated a ranch in Nebraska. For the past several years he had been touring the United States and Canada with his Wild West Show, which drew enormous crowds, particularly in the eastern cities. A Wild West Show was presented in the open air, usually on a fairground where there was plenty of room, and showed white soldiers fighting off the Indians and cowboys rounding up cattle or fighting with rustlers. Another feature of Cody's show was a young woman named Annie Oakley, who was said to be the best rifle shot in the world.

Colonel Cody had served with the cavalry in his

youth but he had a lot of sympathy for the Indians. In fact, he thought they were better to deal with than white people. "The whole secret of getting along with the Indians," he often said, "is to be honest with them and do as you agree."

Until now Sitting Bull didn't believe it was possible for a white man to be honest and live up to his word. However, he liked the frank and open way Buffalo Bill talked and allowed himself to be persuaded to join his show.

All summer Sitting Bull traveled with Cody and the Wild West Show. Many times he was booed and jeered at, since most whites regarded him as the "killer of Custer."

Sitting Bull would ride out into the arena and circle it, listening to the boos and catcalls with a face that showed no sign of emotion. He was being paid well, and he had acquired an appetite for oyster stew and hard candy. As the tour went on, the attitude toward him changed. White people began to see him as the symbol of a defeated enemy who had fought bravely. And everywhere he went crowds surrounded him, particularly children, to shake hands with him and buy his autographed photos.

He kept little of the money he made. Unlike white people, he regarded it as something to be spent or given away as quickly as it was paid over to him.

Annie Oakley, who became a good friend of his, said Sitting Bull couldn't be taught to save.

"Most of what he earned," she said, "went into the pockets of small, ragged boys. White boys. He could not understand why all the wealth he saw in the cities wasn't divided up among the poor. Among the Indians, a man who had plenty of food shared it with those who had none. It was unthinkable for an Indian to feed himself while others were going hungry within eyesight."

Seeing how the whites let their own people stay poor in the midst of plenty convinced Sitting Bull, Annie Oakley said, that they would never do anything for their Indian wards, not if they let their own people go hungry.

"The white man knows how to make everything," he said, "but he does not know how to distribute it."

In Canada, his appearances with Buffalo Bill were even more successful. The Canadians regarded him as a hero for having whipped the Seventh Cavalry. They were naturally more sympathetic toward the Indian. In the first place, they didn't have so many Indians on their hands, and secondly, the Canadian provinces did not attract the millions of immigrants who were coming to the United States and making

William Cody and Sitting Bull

more living space necessary. The Canadians could afford to be more humane, of course, but that does not diminish the fact that they treated their tribes with more understanding and more skill than the Americans did.

The Canadian newspapers said that Sitting Bull "stole the show" and they devoted much more space to him than to Colonel Cody himself. Speeches were made in the Canadian Parliament when the show appeared in Ottawa, in which Sitting Bull was hailed as "the illustrious Indian general and statesman."

At the end of the season Sitting Bull went back to the Standing Rock Reservation with a huge white sombrero, which Buffalo Bill had given him and which he wore only on important occasions.

In 1887 Colonel Cody took his show to England during Queen Victoria's Jubilee. He wanted Sitting Bull to go along, and so did Major McLaughlin, the Indian agent at Standing Rock, who was always glad to see the back of the troublesome chief. But Sitting Bull refused. He no longer wanted to make a show of himself for the white people. All their applause meant no more to him than their jeers.

"It is bad for our cause for me to parade around," he said. "It awakens the hatred of white people everywhere. Besides, I am needed here."

He saw that he must live not only for himself but as the leader of his people. He must provide an example for them. So instead of going to England and being presented to "Grandmother," Queen Victoria, and being flattered and lionized by dukes and princes, he stayed on the reservation.

It was plain that he and the Sioux would have to walk the "white man's road," as they called it, so he had decided they must make the best of it. If Indians were supposed to be farmers, he would show them it could be done. He moved to a patch of land on the Grand River near where he had been born, lived in a log cabin, began raising cattle and chickens, and tilled his corn patch. All he asked now was that the white man build a school for the children of his tribe so they could learn to make their way in a white man's world.

But that didn't mean that he was willing to give in to any demands the white man made upon him. In the summer of 1889 his old enemy, General Crook, came to Standing Rock at the head of a commission that wanted to buy up more of the little land left to the Sioux for their reservation. If the Sioux chief did not agree, it was hinted, his people's rations would be reduced. Sitting Bull wouldn't consider giving up any more land.

The commission, through Major McLaughlin,

then went behind Sitting Bull's back and made a deal with his rival, John Grass, by which the lands were handed over. Sitting Bull protested but it did no good. The matter was settled at a council to which Sitting Bull was not invited.

When he heard how the deal had been worked, Sitting Bull commented to his friend, Circling Hawk: "They have finished us now. I understand why they wanted me to go to England. They wanted to get our lands while I was gone. It took them longer when I refused to go, but they have succeeded. The great Sioux Nation is a thing of the past. Without land, we are nothing."

Within a few years, the government had succeeded in shrinking the Sioux lands from a territory that stretched over several future states of the Union, to a large reservation, and finally to a very small reservation.

TEN

The Ghost Dancers

IN THE SPRING OF 1889 an apparition appeared at
the Standing Rock Agency. To the surprise
and horror of all the white people there, the Indian Bureau officials, the army officers and their
wives, a white woman had come out from the East
determined to help the Indians. Such a thing was
unheard of. Women in that time were supposed to
think of nothing but their homes and husbands.
Now here was this strange female from Brooklyn,
who came to Dakota Territory proclaiming that she
intended to help Sitting Bull save his people.

Sixty years later women of the same kind would
be marching in southern cities in defense of Negro
civil rights—but this was 1889 and woman's place, as

she was told so often, particularly by her menfolk, was "in the home."

The woman who came out to help Sitting Bull was Mrs. Catherine Weldon. She was in her late forties, good-looking, well-dressed, and a widow. What made her even more an object of suspicion was that she was an artist.

Yet the people at Standing Rock couldn't turn her away. She was a representative of the National Indian Defense Association and she had a right to be there.

Major McLaughlin tried his best to talk her out of seeing Sitting Bull. He told her, as she later recalled, that the great chief was "a coward, a savage, one who hated all white people and would do them harm if he got the chance."

She replied that she had come out to the Dakotas to help the Sioux and would wait there at the agency until Sitting Bull came to see her.

The chief drove forty miles in a horse and buggy from his farm on the Grand River to meet Mrs. Weldon.

Sitting Bull realized that Mrs. Weldon had come to help him and his people, and he even hoped that she might be able to influence Washington against taking more of their land away. Perhaps she could persuade Grandfather to change his mind about the deal signed by John Grass, which turned over so much more land to the government.

Mrs. Weldon was greatly impressed the moment she met Sitting Bull by his grave and dignified manner. She told him that other whites at the agency warned her that he might kidnap her and keep her as a white squaw.

"I look upon you as my own daughter," Sitting Bull said of that warning, "and I will protect you as I would a daughter."

He invited her to come to his farm, and Mrs. Weldon agreed. Major McLaughlin was shocked and outraged by her acceptance, as were all the other whites at Standing Rock. They caused a story to be published in the newspapers saying that Mrs. Weldon had come out to marry Sitting Bull. Regarding that published lie, Mrs. Weldon later wrote: "All this is the agent's [Major McLaughlin's] work. He fears Sitting Bull's influence among his people and therefore pretends to his face that my welfare was his concern, and he took the opportunity to humble the old chief and make his heart more than sad. In order to lessen my influence as a member of the National Indian Defense Association, he makes me ridiculous by having the story printed. Is there no protection for defenseless women?"

Even Sitting Bull misunderstood her brave, well-meaning intentions. She moved into his house, considered herself a member of his family, and helped with the housekeeping chores. To Sitting Bull that signified, as the Indians understood such matters, that she wanted to be his squaw.

"Chaska," he said, referring to another Sioux, "has married a white woman."

Mrs. Weldon was surprised and outraged at his offer to make her his wife. He already had a wife. "You had no business to tell me of Chaska," she told him, as she later recalled in her account of her life in Sitting Bull's household. "Is this the reward for the friendship which I have proved to you?"

Finally she managed to convince Sitting Bull that she hadn't come out to the village on the Grand River to become his wife, but was there to help him and his people because she thought they were being shamefully mistreated.

And she did help in every way she could. She provided money for Sitting Bull to appeal his case against the latest land seizure and paid for maps of the reservation to be drawn, boundaries surveyed, and the holdings of each family listed. She also went back East for several months to enlist the support of her friends in Sitting Bull's cause and wrote articles about the Indians' plight. The Indian Bureau had not only failed to keep its promises after taking more of the Sioux lands but actually cut their rations by another 20 per cent. There was hunger and starvation at the Pine Ridge and Standing Rock agencies. A drought made it impossible for good crops to be harvested in the fall of 1889.

The Sioux were desperate, but Mrs. Weldon's tireless efforts could do little to help them. In a way, her presence in Sitting Bull's household only made things worse. The notion of a white woman living voluntarily among the "savages" only made Major McLaughlin and other government officials raging mad.

The whites' anger was soon reinforced by fear. The Ghost Dance came to the Sioux agencies in Dakota Territory.

It was a new religion, one that stirred up the Indians on reservations all over the West. An Indian prophet named Wovoka, who lived in Nevada, announced that Jesus Christ had returned to earth, this time in the person of an Indian. The whites had killed Him on his first appearance on earth. Now He had come to save the Indians from their despair. The Messiah would bring back all the Indian dead and all the buffalo that had disappeared with the coming of the white man. The Messiah would also give the Indians their land back and would remove all the white men from the North American continent.

To make all this come true, the Indians were supposed to hold Ghost Dances endlessly around their camp fires. Sometimes the Ghost Dancers stomped in their unbroken circle for two days and two nights at a time. They would drop in exhaustion and see visions of the new Messiah, of their dead coming back to life, of the buffalo returning.

The Ghost Dance craze reached the Sioux reservation in October of 1890. Many of the Sioux joined the new faith, which was really the Christian religion adapted to Indian purposes, Indian longings, and privations.

Sitting Bull was asked to join the Ghost Dancers but he refused. The old religion of the Indians—faith in the Great Manitou and all the other Indian gods—was good enough for him. He was too old for new ideas.

Catherine Weldon preached against the Ghost Dancers. She told the Sioux it was all nonsense and that they would be hurt by it in the end. The whites were greatly alarmed by the swift spread of the Ghost Dance cult, and newspapers were filled with reports that it was a mask for a new uprising. If it weren't stopped, it might give the army an

Wovoka and the Ghost Dancers

excuse for stepping in and bringing the Indians under even tighter control.

Mrs. Weldon also begged Sitting Bull to stop the Ghost Dancing, to use his influence among the Sioux against it.

"The younger ones no longer listen to me," he said. "They join the Indian Police. They join the Ghost Dancers. They do as they please. I do not believe in the Ghost Dance myself, but I cannot prevent my people from believing as they choose. If it gives them hope, who am I to talk against it? The government takes away their food, but I will not take away their hope."

"You known what it means?" Mrs. Weldon demanded. "The soldiers will come. The whites are frightened by the Ghost Dance, it awakens all the feelings of guilt in them, and they cannot bear to have the Christian religion turned against them. That will make them cruel. You must stop your people from provoking a reaction from the army."

"I have fought the whites' army all my life," he replied, "but I cannot fight this religion. It means nothing to me, but I will not interfere with other people's beliefs."

The leader of the Ghost Dancers among the Sioux was Kicking Bear, who saw the new faith as a means of gaining power and prestige among his people. Mrs. Weldon challenged him to appear with her in a debate over the Ghost Dance, but he refused to meet her.

The Indians would not listen, so she swallowed her pride and wrote long letters to Major McLaughlin begging him to adopt a more understanding attitude.

"Have pity on the Hunkpapa and other Sioux who have been listening to Kicking Bear," she wrote the Indian Bureau's head man at Standing Rock. "Do not send police or soldiers! My heart is almost breaking when I see the work of years undone. . . . It was money, health and heart thrown away. . . ."

Possibly at Mrs. Weldon's urging, McLaughlin went to talk to Sitting Bull about the Ghost Dance.

"You do not understand this dance," Sitting Bull told Major McLaughlin. "But I am willing to be convinced. You and I will go together to the tribes in the West, where the Ghost Dance began. We will ask that they show us the Messiah. If we do not find the Messiah, and the dead coming back to life, and the buffalo returning, then you and I will come back here and tell the Sioux it is all a lie. That will end the Dance. If we find the Messiah, the Dance will go on."

It was a fair proposition, but McLaughlin said he didn't have the time or money to go on the trip to Nevada.

Instead he recruited new young men for his Indian Police. The army began preparing for a campaign against the Sioux and any other Indians who persisted in Ghost Dancing. In the East it was so obvious that the government was getting ready to punish the Indians once again—though the Ghost Dancers had not commited a single act of violence—that friends of the Indians began trying to head off another Indian war.

Buffalo Bill Cody, in Chicago, heard that the army might move against Sitting Bull and the Sioux. He hurried to the Standing Rock Agency and bought a wagon load of gifts for the old chief, intending to persuade him to use his influence against the Ghost Dancing. Colonel Cody also heard that the government was planning to arrest Sitting Bull. He knew that his old friend would resist, and there would be shooting. The whites would be only too happy if Sitting Bull were killed in the process.

Buffalo Bill started out for Sitting Bull's village on the Grand River but was halted by Major McLaughlin, who assured him that the order for Sitting Bull's arrest had been rescinded.

It was getting late in the year 1890 and the Ghost

Dance craze was dying out among the Sioux, but Sitting Bull felt doom in his old bones. He knew that the young Sioux who had joined Major McLaughlin's Indian Police were eager to prove themselves great men by arresting or killing the old war chief who had once led all the Plains Indians in battle. He was particularly wary of a young man named Bullhead, who had been made lieutenant of the Indian Police.

It wasn't the white man's army he feared now, but people of his own blood. It made him sad and bitter to think the Sioux could be turned against him this way by money, honors, flattery, whiskey. He thought back to the day of the Battle of the Little Big Horn when he had warned his people against taking the slain white soldiers' possessions because they would be corrupted by them. So it had happened.

One day he was out looking for his old white horse, which was hiding from him in the brush, when he heard a meadowlark singing. Once again —like the yellow bird in his youth—the Bird People were warning him.

The meadowlark, he later told his friends, was singing:

"The Sioux will kill you."

[133]

Death Comes in the Night

O N DECEMBER 11, 1890, Sitting Bull made a last
effort to come to peaceful terms with the Indian Bureau and its chief agent on the reservation,
Major McLaughlin, by dictating a letter to him
through a young Sioux in his village who had learned
to read and write in the school Sitting Bull had persuaded the government to build.

"God made you—made all the white race, and also
made the red race—and gave them both might and
heart to know everything in the world, but gave the
whites the advantage over the Indians. . . . I wish
no man to come to me in my prayers with gun or
knife. . . . You should say nothing against our religion, for we said nothing against yours. . . . You pray
to God, so do all of us Indians. . . . We both pray to

one God, who made us all. . . . You don't like me because you think I am a fool, and you imagine that, if I were not here, all the Indians would become civilized, and that, because I am here, all the Indians are fools. . . . I am obliged to go to Pine Ridge Agency to investigate this Ghost Dance religion. So I write to let you know that."

For once Sitting Bull did not express himself clearly, but it was apparent to anyone who was capable of understanding that the old chief wanted peace and was willing to do anything he could to bring it about.

His message reached Major McLaughlin the next day, December 12, but it was too late even if the major were willing to listen to reason. The army, a few hours earlier, had sent McLaughlin an order for Sitting Bull's arrest.

There would be bloodshed. The Sioux would react violently to Sitting Bull's arrest or killing, even if many of the young men had gone over to the whites. And Sitting Bull had nothing to do with the unrest caused by the Ghost Dance. The government, however, was going ahead with its plan to eliminate Sitting Bull once and for all as an influence over his people.

Major McLaughlin decided that Sitting Bull's letter, in any case, was a trick—he just wanted a pass to leave his village, and then he would go around the reservation stirring up his tribesmen to fight against the whites! The major might have held up the arrest, but Sitting Bull's well-meant letter, its intentions misread by the man it was appealing to, caused McLaughlin to take action immediately.

Lieutenant Bullhead and his Indian Police were sent to Sitting Bull's village to bring the old chief to the agency headquarters at Standing Rock.

Meanwhile, reports that Sitting Bull would be arrested sped around the whole reservation. Some of his warriors, now grown old with him, and Jumping Bull, his adopted brother, headed for Sitting Bull's village, swearing they would protect him from the Indian Police.

They arrived at Sitting Bull's small farm on the evening of December 13. Sitting Bull was calm, ready for anything that might happen. He ordered his squaws to prepare a meal for all his old friends, and introduced them to his son, Crowfoot, who was seventeen years old and going to school to learn how to live the white man's way. After the meal, Sitting Bull stuffed kinnikinnick (a form of tobacco) into his huge old pipe and passed it around the circle of his friends squatting on the floor of his house. They talked of the old days, when they were free, of the battles they had won, and of the great hunts and Sun Dances.

All night they talked, and at daybreak Sitting Bull told them to go back to their homes.

"I do not need to be guarded," he told his friends. "You can go home now. I know you sympathize with me, but go home and give water and feed to your cattle."

They did as he ordered, but later that day, December 14, they returned to Sitting Bull's house. Once again they ate with him, smoked kinnikinnick, and talked of old times, but they also kept listening for sounds outside—sounds of the approach of Sitting Bull's enemies.

That night they all slept in a small cabin next to Sitting Bull's house.

An hour before daylight there was a drumming of horses' hoofs on the frozen surface of the road leading up from the river. Lieutenant Bullhead and his second-in-command, Sergeant Shavehead, and forty members of the Indian Police were charging up the road toward Sitting Bull's house.

They broke in the door, and two of the police grabbed Sitting Bull before he could reach for the carbine and knife he kept under the blankets. In a moment the cabin was full of police.

[137]

Sitting Bull began struggling to free himself of the police hanging onto his arms. It took three of the young Sioux police to hold him down. His friends rushed over from the cabin next door.

"If you fight," Lieutenant Bullhead shouted in the darkness, "you will all be killed."

Someone lit a kerosene lamp, and Sitting Bull's friends could see him struggling with his captors. It was an explosive situation. All the Indian Police were heavily armed. Many of Sitting Bull's friends and fellow villagers had rifles. It was dark in the cabin, lit only by one lamp, and everyone was excited.

"Get your clothes on!" Lieutenant Bullhead told Sitting Bull. "We are taking you to Standing Rock under arrest."

An Indian Police sergeant named Red Tomahawk was standing behind Sitting Bull. He jabbed his revolver into Sitting Bull's back and ordered him to hurry up.

The old chief was surrounded by Indian Police trying to rush him out the door, but they were blocked by Sitting Bull's friends.

"Shoot the officers," one of Sitting Bull's old warriors shouted, "and all the younger ones will run away."

Sitting Bull himself, enraged at the way he was being prodded, pushed, and hauled around, suddenly shouted above the din, "I'm not going! Get away from me! Get away!"

Jumping Bull, his adopted brother, feared that the Indian Police would start shooting. He was certain they would kill Sitting Bull if he attempted to resist arrest. All they needed was an excuse to start firing their new Winchester repeating rifles.

He forced his way to Sitting Bull's side and urged him to stay calm. "Do not fight with them, brother. Go to the agency with them. I will take my family and you will take yours to Standing Rock. If you are to die there, I will die with you."

"That's right," Lieutenant Bullhead said. "Come along peacefully. Tell your people to stand back."

But Sitting Bull wouldn't give the order. He wasn't going to be hauled away from his home and put in the white man's jail.

One of his followers let out a war whoop. Catch-a-Bear, an old friend of Sitting Bull's, fired point-blank at Lieutenant Bullhead and shot him in the chest, near the heart. Then everyone started shooting.

The Indian Police and the Hunkpapa shot it out right there in the cabin and just outside, where Sitting Bull's followers were milling around and trying to get to his side. It was a slaughter on both sides, everyone firing blindly in the dim light.

Lieutenant Bullhead was lying mortally wounded on the floor. With his last breath he was determined to take Sitting Bull with him. He took out his revolver and fired upward, just once.

Sitting Bull fell dead with a bullet in his heart, killed by one of his own people, just as the meadowlark had warned him.

In the next few moments of blind fury, many others fell. It was probably the wildest gun battle ever seen in the Old West. When it was over, within fifty yards of each other, a score were dead or dying on both sides. Along with Sitting Bull, his adopted brother Jumping Bull and his seventeen-year-old son Crowfoot, nine other Hunkpapas lay, dead; two others were dying of their wounds, and another was seriously wounded. Four Indian Police were killed, and Lieutenant Bullhead and Sergeant Shavehead would die of their wounds within a few hours.

The surviving police sent a message to a troop of U.S. cavalry standing by a few miles away. The white cavalrymen came riding up and arrested all the surviving members of Sitting Bull's village.

But that was only the beginning of the killing and suffering of Sitting Bull's people.

All the Sioux were ordered by the army to come to the Standing Rock and Pine Ridge agencies and surrender all their weapons. Many did as they ordered, but others were hunted down and shot when they attempted to escape from the ring of cavalry that surrounded the reservation. On the morning of December 28, two weeks after Sitting Bull's death, one village of Sioux was surrounded by a regiment that had been smarting for fourteen years from the memory of the Little Big Horn. The village wasn't quick enough about surrendering, so the Seventh Cavalry opened fire with machine guns, cannon, and rifles.

They called it the "battle" of Wounded Knee Creek in the records, but it was no battle. It was a massacre. One hundred and twenty-six Sioux men, women, and children were hunted down over the snow-covered prairie and killed. That was the official report. One general, however, admitted that at least 200 were killed. Unofficially, it was reported by newspaper correspondents that the cavalrymen used fleeing Indian women and children for target practice.

It was the last battle ever fought between the

white man's army and the Indians. Just how over-whelming the odds were against the Indians is indicated by the fact that the army had gathered together more than 8,000 soldiers to put down an "uprising" by a few thousand half-starved Sioux.

Probably if Sitting Bull had been able to foresee what suffering his last struggle against the white man would cause, he would not have resisted the Indian Police. He was always thinking of his people's welfare, but the meadowlark who warned him that he would be killed by fellow Sioux didn't tell him that a greater horror would follow.

His death was that of a great chief fighting with his last breath for freedom. To his people he left a legend that still sustains them on their reservation in South Dakota, and to the world—to all of us—he left the example of one man who would die rather than submit to what he believed was wrong.

INDEX

[143]